The seeker for truth and for
contact with the hierarchy of light
and the Great White Brotherhood
must, of necessity, come directly
under the aegis and guidance of the
great master teachers. To embark
on the path toward mastery, achievement, victory, and the ascension
is an initiatic process. Whether it be
Zarathustra who ascended back to
God in "the great flame," or Elijah
who went into heaven in the "chariot
of fire," the flame of the ascension
is the key which unlocks the door
to immortality for every man.

—SERAPIS BEY

The Sensings of Serapis

From the Teacher and the Teaching of the Path of the Sphinx and the Great Pyramid

Peace from the heart of Luxor.

I heard the discipline of God and I perceived it as the manifestation of his order. Out of the chaos and dimension of mortal mind and confusion, I perceived the luminous orb of Christed intelligence strike as from the star Draconis deep onto the pyramidal line.

And I saw the Chamber of the King. And I saw the Chamber of the Queen. And I saw the pyramid of lives. And I saw the Master Mason draw his line.

And I saw the security of the divine geometry. I saw the cubit stone. And I saw the measure of a man. And I saw how that every man must strive to fit the master plan. And knowledge was needed and a torch. And the chamber must be traversed, and initiation must come. And man must pass from death unto life.

For the sun and the moon and the stars and the luminous orbs of creation are concentric focuses, orbs of light, masses of light, masses of energy, of density, of outpicturization.

And man is so and knows it not.

For the whirling galaxy within is also under dominion.

And as a ship without rudder or compass or captain, so do compassless lives cross uncharted seas and individuals are lost, hearing not the voice of the Ancient Mariner and the voice of Truth that parts the veil of mortal lies and leads men to pass from the bondage of Egypt, across the Red Sea, beyond the desert of Sinai, and into the land of promise.

It is most unfortunate but it is true that in the disciplines of men their hearts are often so familiar with the cadences and lines of truth that scar tissue has formed upon the seat of consciousness within them until they can no longer derive satisfaction from the holy tenets of our faith. And our faith is in purpose.

And men must learn to still the mind as one would grasp a blade of steel and thrust it not forward one quarter of an inch until the command to do battle was given. A soldier exercises control and heeds the call of the captain. . . .

The cone of fire pulsates from dullness to the brilliance of the white light, and the residual ash is consumed itself. And the egg of the serpent must not be left, for it can well bring forth not only a serpent or a sea serpent but a dragon. And thus the cone of fire must be preserved until the blinding light of transposition, of transmutation does consume the dross and produce the fruit of the Cosmic Egg.

The ovoid of the Infinite is within the capacity of mortal men. But then, when invoked, they are no longer mortal. But immortality is of high price, and it demands the allness of men from the smallness of men. . . .

The very power of the mind of God which framed the world was to draw energy into a cohesive whole so that design by universal law could manifest through a cosmic geometry as all of the myriad forces of nature with their many patterns—helixes, cones, squares, circles, and many other geometric figures.

The use to which nature has put all of these various geometrical forms ought to show mankind that the mind of God has indeed drawn upon the knowledge of cosmic geometry to produce in the world of form a perfection of order which is very beautiful in structure. Contemplation of that by mankind ought to show that no happenstance was involved in the mysteries of creation but only a magnificent pattern of delight and order and intent and purpose.

If this purpose manifests as the harmony of nature, then this purpose, as order and discipline in the lives of the aspirants who would have their ascension, must come forth now.

I am speaking now to individuals throughout the planetary body who are not attendant here at Luxor but who desire to matriculate along the same lines as our chelas do here and participate in their own ascension at the close of this embodiment. To you I say, a more than ordinary discipline must be given. . . .

Guard, then, your harmony that the cone may have little residual ash, that the dragon's tooth will not be found within the dragon's egg. . . .

Men cannot build out of mortal substance immortal bodies. They cannot build out of mortal thoughts immortal ideas. They cannot build out of mortal feelings divine feelings that enfold the world and create the great Pyramid of Life.

The great Pyramid of Life stems from the giant square of the Divine Architect's mind, a mind that has all right angles and produces out of the four corners of substance the beauty of perfection rising from the spheres of mortal dimension.

Let men understand the meaning of this, for the base of life is in form but ariseth out of form. The social order, the order of individuals, the order of nations, the order of hierarchy—all orders are constructed geometrically. And the cubit stones that compose these divisions, becoming then unifications through cohesive force, are held together by the power of love that deems no sacrifice too great. . . .

The science behind the ascension is very great indeed. And the contributions necessary by mankind to the world order would build in the world order a pillar of great beauty, a pyramid of lives in harmony, a pyramid of architectural grandeur.

Then the greensward will stretch toward the four corners of the earth. Then the Pyramid will glow. Then the fire of the Spirit will transmute first the base stones, and the capstone will be the last to glow. For all energy in the capstone is from on high and that which is in the base is from below.

But the qualifications of the base must conform, by reason of thought and devotion, to the pattern from on high. And thus the fire will be drawn down first to the base stones.

And then the capstone supported by the base stones will glow as the sweep of the great electronic stream from the heart of God moves down symmetrically and in perfect divine order through the entire structure, causing the Pyramid to glow on the greensward.

And it will come to pass that, with the accomplishment of the capstone crowning man's achievement, the civilization of the golden age, the permanent golden age will begin.

And then the destiny of America and of the world will be outpictured because the pyramid of lives will have adjusted itself in conformity to divine principle.

And the Grand Mason of the Universe, the Eternal God, will himself express satisfaction by causing to descend out of heaven the hand that carries the torch.

And when this occurs, that which is below will manifest that which is above. . . .

I am Serapis. I have known the scenes of earth. I have known setbacks and I have known the strengthening whereby every loss has become an impetus for gain. . . .

I am known as the Disciplinarian, and working with me at Luxor are 144 instructors in the Temple of the Ascension where candidates are received each week who desire to serve a period of internship, of preparation for the ascension.

These are they who have walked the earth in the service of the Christ, in the service of the Buddha, in the service of God in man—whether tutored by ministers, by rabbis, by counselors, by priests, or devotees of the mystery schools.

For we measure candidates for the ascension by the action of God's holy will in life, by the action of God's holy wisdom in life, by the action of God's holy love in life. And discipline is our byword. . . .

Let the strings of the soul be taut for the striking by the hand of the Master Harpist. Let the strings of the soul be God-taught. Let them be disciplined in the sacred fire, pitched at the point of celestial harmony.

The geometry of the soul is impelled into manifestation by discipline. And so I come, sent by God, as the Guru of initiates of the sacred fire.

If you would wait a million years for mastery, go find another. For Serapis is impatient for perfection....

Perfection is a tangible reality here and now.

I think that those who think they cannot be perfect imagine that perfection is a straitjacket or a sterile quality lacking any verve or energy or joy or spontaneity. Nay, perfection is the flowering of the lilies, of the gentle violets. Perfection is a smile upon a face.

God does not measure perfection by human standards. After all, how can the human have a standard of perfection? God measures the motive in the heart, the love in the heart. And that which mankind criticize, God ennobles as perfection.

God is not concerned whether or not the drawing of the little child is letter-perfect according to the great artists of the times. God is concerned that the little hand has drawn a flower as the little heart has seen the flower....

I am Serapis. I see the need for disciplined ones. And I see the futility of superimposing discipline upon the unwilling consciousness. Only love can draw forth from within your being the necessary components to your ascension. You cannot love yourself more than God....

We need not complicate cosmic law. Cosmic law is love in action. Cosmic love is law in action. Cosmic love and law are your faith, your hope, your joy....

And if you could see all that heaven holds in store for you, you would be swift and take the wings of the eagles to fly into our retreats in the highest crannies of the mountains. You would come, you would run from your earthly involvements. You would not tarry in Terra, you would rise and rise and rise on the fountain of light within. And then you would bring forth fruits of innovation, creativity, newness, ideas, blueprints—oh, so many wonders that the children of mankind are waiting to know and to hear about....

To serve the Christ in all is to receive the reward of the Christ. To that end, I discipline. To that end, I initiate. And I am concerned with the top flight, the gold of consciousness....

If you would be initiated then I say, be willing to come

to the feet of your own reality first. Then be willing to accept that there is a reality which God has vested in beings, in masters who have gone beyond this phase and this plane, who have a greater grasp of the Real Self than you now do though you have equal opportunity to attain that grasp.

They have reached for the Infinite and they have won. But they look back and extend a hand, for they won by love for humanity.

Therefore I say, take the hand of hierarchy. Take the hand extended. Walk slow or swiftly but walk with measured beat, steady in the rhythm of your own Reality.

Press toward the mark and the prize of the high calling—the calling of the law of your inner Self. And know that if you would attain swiftly, I am there to impel you forward. I am there with the sword of the ascension flame. . . .

I am Serapis.

Dossier on the Ascension

Ascension

Serapis Bey

The Story of the Soul's Acceleration
into Higher Consciousness
on the Path of Initiation

recorded by
Mark L. Prophet

DOSSIER ON THE ASCENSION: *The Story of the Soul's Acceleration into Higher Consciousness on the Path of Initiation* by Serapis Bey recorded by Mark L. Prophet. Copyright © 1967, 1978 Summit University Press. All rights reserved.

Cover by Norman Thomas Miller
Serapis Bey receives a neophyte into the mystery school of the Sphinx and the Great Pyramid

Library of Congress Catalog Card Number: 76-28088
ISBN: 0-916766-21-7

SUMMIT UNIVERSITY ♆ PRESS ®
Summit University Press and ♆ are registered trademarks.

This book is set in Paladium.
Printed in the United States of America
First Printing 1979. Second Printing 1980. Third Printing 1984
Fourth Printing 1986. Fifth Printing 1988. Sixth Printing 1993
Seventh Printing 1995

To preserve the Teachings of the Ascended Masters for posterity, this book has been printed on acid-free paper that meets the requirements of ANSI/NISO Z39.48-1992 (Permanence of Paper). This paper is rated to last several hundred years without significant deterioration under archival storage conditions.

Contents

1

The Reality
of the
Inner Walk with God

Unto You
Who Remember
the Ancient of Days:
Greetings from the
Brotherhood at Luxor
Who Keep the Memory
of His Sacred Name

The sling of David shows what man can do when he is wedded by faith to his own latent divinity.[1] The mimicry of humanity abounds in the world, and while imitation may be the highest form of flattery, the question before the hierarchy is "What do the current models offer?"

Men must return to the pristine, to the reality of the inner walk with God, to the high temple magic embodied and captured by living truth. The world media proclaim the wares of mankind that material treasures may be bolstered, but seldom do men hear the voice that cries in the wilderness proclaiming to make straight the way of the Lord.[2] Almost forgotten are the sweet lispings "Train up a child in the way he should go: and when he is old, he will not depart from it."[3]

I, Serapis, then, do come in memory of the Ancient of Days[4] and in memory of the heritage of mankind which is not crucifixion, albeit men die daily,[5] nor resurrection, although some men are transformed daily, but is that splendid finale of the ascension. When men sail, going abroad, those upon the shore gaily wave to those aboard ship. With the moving out of the ship to sea, there is a happy separation and thought of reunion. So should it be with those whose departing does leave behind them golden footsteps pointing toward Cycles' heritage. Not death, not even separation is reality, but ascension's currents residual within all men in whom dwells the seed of God.

Is it not clearly recorded that upon the Tree of Life twelve manner of fruit should appear?[6] And is it not recorded that when the Master Jesus anointed the eyes of the blind man that his first impression was "I see men as trees, walking"?[7] What is the mystery, then, of the spinal tree behind the spine, of the sympathetic nervous system and the ganglionic trunks over which flow the currents of immortal life? How is the Deathless Solar Body fabricated and from whence is spun the substance of the wedding garment?[8]

Does not all come through the alchemy of the self, and in a very real sense did not God ordain that every man should become his own Saviour? Oh, we are not talking about paltry mortal flesh and blood. We are not talking about the finite man. We are talking about the God-man, the Presence of Life that is the individualized reality of every soul. The Presence of God individualized as true being is "I AM." This is that flaming Spirit— deathless, birthless, uncreated and yet creating— that spake to Moses out of the flaming fire in the bush, saying, "I AM THAT I AM."[9]

The mystery of the ascension, then, is attained by partaking of the Tree of Life and the twelve manner of fruit thereof. It is attained by the realization of the Real Man. Men do not gather grapes of thistles and no matter how many wolves may parade in sheep's clothing[10] and sing forth high-sounding phrases which become no more than a "tinkling cymbal,"[11] the law of God cannot be broken with impunity and the watermarks of man's rebellion and confusion rise high in the astral record, signifying man's lack of emotional control.

Some have met with our lieutenants, our codirectors at Luxor, who greet the young neophytes as they arrive. Some have commented on what they have termed the lack of feeling, the lack of emotion, and even the lack of love our representatives have expressed. They have not understood that love is not just a feeling, an "emoting" that desires to swallow up the object of its affection. Those who hallow space understand why the planets are placed in orbits allowing *lebensraum* (living room) for each orb to circulate in the dignity of self-manifestation. True love is love for the God flame and holds no other desire save the expectation of the amplification of that flame as a tangible, divine feeling that sweeps the world pure and clean "with the washing of the water by the Word" invincible.[12]

The purification of the soul in the ritual of the ascension must be recognized as the manifestation of that pristine and original ideation of God which men call the 'soul'. The real meaning of the soul is "Solar-El," which refers to the latent power of the divine angel within man.[13] (I do not expect that all of my words will be interpreted correctly nor that they will be understood by all, but I must state the law in order that those who have been initiated to a level of comprehension suitable for the revelation inherent within this mystery may then comprehend it.) The Solar-El is the infinite idea of God projected by the divine light through the so-called seven densities of creation, including the angelic realm and evolving within man as the evolution of divine energy intended in the beginning.

One of the saddest ideas in connection with the ascension is that those who are accustomed to rock 'n' roll, Wiener schnitzel, egoistic bolstering, and the suave distinction and glorification of the lesser self may actually fear the abolishment of that which they hold dear as spelling an end to their individual worlds. These live in a lilliputian world which has meaning and depth to them because of their habit patterns of long standing and their mimicry of that which seems to be a pleasant idea to the mortal mind.

We seek to raise the veil upon the wonderful world of cosmic magic, the magic of believing in the power of the original intent which may then be blazed as the all-consuming love of God through the entire warp and woof of the self. Changes will be wrought, of course. They should be expected. But we who know every step of the way say to you all, they will be welcomed changes once the soul becomes acclimatized and the consciousness adjusted to its new environment.

Naturally there will be a space, an increment of time between the opening of the first seal of reality and the fulmination of that magical potion, the elixir of Life, into the test tube of the human soul. How could it be otherwise? For certainly that which men deem to be life and hold to be real, while it holds a semblance of reality is not the reality with which God will bless mankind. Nevertheless, men must understand that the springboard of the present life is a platform upon which the cosmic astronaut will be launched into higher dimensions.

We at Luxor are not without a "contactual" love for everyone who comes to us and seeks to amplify the ascension currents. We simply dare not recognize the stratum of the human emanation that layer upon layer has imprudently builded out of pure light substance, causing shadowed enclosures to surround the Self of man in concentric rings of error.

Error produces pain and suffering. We who understand the correct use of energy must, then, greet the chela in what appears to be an impersonal manner but which in actuality is an intense focusing of the God flame within ourselves in the God flame within the aspirant. We have seen cases where for over forty years we have focused this flame within an individual before securing results. Then in an instant, in the twinkling of an eye, a God is born![14] Some have within a period of forty days of purification come to the position of Christhood and readied themselves for the ascension.

Let love, then, be indeed without dissimulation[15] and be not carried away by those who gush over mankind in order to win him over to mortal thoughts and feelings. Our laws are perfect laws and they can never be flaunted. They are embodied within the Spirit of the flame at Luxor. May I carry on in the coming week and tell you more? For your freedom and victory, I AM

Your brother at Luxor,

Serapis

2

"When We Have Shuffled Off This Mortal Coil"

Unto You
Who Recoil Not from
Ascension's Coil
but Would Be Recoiled
in the Sacred Fire—
I AM Come to Transfer
the Compressed Energy
of My Causal Body

In continuing my dissertation on the ascension, which is the gift of God for all, I take you now to the Shakespearean plays and to the statement made

> To sleep! perchance to dream—
>   ay, there's the rub;
> For in that sleep of death
>   what dreams may come,
> When we have shuffled off
>   this mortal coil,
> Must give us pause:[1]

Seekers for freedom and truth, know that the play of the emotions and the fire of the mind are determinant in creating the record referred to in *Hamlet* as "this mortal coil." For around the body and being of man, energy, compressed energy—like a giant spring wrapped, in some cases, unmercifully tight and, in other cases, loosely knit—does exist. This coil governs the amount of time and energy required by each lifestream actually to cut himself free from misguided effort.

Because individuals by divine grace and mercy have hidden from their own eyes the extent of the degradation to which they have fallen in their total schema of past embodiments, I would suggest that it is preferable for everyone to feel that the weight of his karma is less rather than gross. For when individuals who have what we would call a heavy karma become obsessed with the idea of that karma, they create a certain lethargy in their feelings and an almost unwillingness to begin paying off the karmic debt, feeling that it is too overpowering even to contemplate.

When individuals believe their karma to be very light and they enter into the spirit of releasing it swiftly into the sacred fire, there is a great release of joy that flows through their beings. The action of joy has a tendency to create malleability in the coils of energy, a relaxing of the tensions inherent within these energetic coils, and the freeing of the individual from restless tides which have, over the centuries, proved to be his nemesis. In seeking, then, the ascension in the light, the power of love must be recognized as a fervent heat which will cause the elements of mortal creation to melt and the very being of man to meld into a great pool of cosmic light and love.

Now because of man's intently conceived ideas about life and love, there is always the danger that individuals will overpower the truth that lies behind the worded symbol by their own shallowness of concept and thus fail to acquire the power of the Word that went forth on behalf of their own freedom and quickening.

The giant storings retained within the heart of the Christ as he lay within the tomb were the results of no idle effort. They were the power of universal law and life, of enormous concentration of resurrection's flame, and of the receptivity of the chalice of his great heart of faith that in olden days did in golden cadences sweetly say, "Thou wilt not leave my soul in hell; nor suffer thine Holy One to see corruption."[2]

Men must come to understand that it is the poison of mortal concepts that has created the sting of death, that the strength of sin lies within the law[3] and that this law man has made to read, "In sin did my mother conceive me,"[4] while denying the immortal birthright of the heavenly Father who can justly say of all his creation, "Ye are my offspring."

If you are the offspring of God, then there should be resident within you the "dayspring from on high,"[5] the energetic coil of the Spirit of the resurrection and the ascension out of human density and patterns of lethargy. While it is unquestionably true that a plant can split a rock by the power of Life within the root of the plant, it of necessity requires greater energy for it to accomplish this feat. If the rock is not in the way, then only the gentle earth needs to be moved.

Thus let me clearly declare that the stripping away of the coils of negative energy surrounding mankind, the yielding up of old and residual ideas that have not brought to man his freedom, and the substitution of great positivity of mind does help to remove the crushing weight of human effluvia from the soul and prepares the way for Christly vestments to be placed about the shoulders of the neophyte, of the seeker for greater light.

Candidates for the ascension understand the plan that surely as He has measured the everlasting hills, surely as He has prepared a place for those who love Him, the way is made plain that either men continue to dwell in the darkness of mortal concepts and misunderstandings, culminating in the death of the body and the release of the soul, or they accept the opportunities which life offers them and become candidates for the ascension. Those who do so welcome the surge of the ascension flame through their minds and bodies, for they understand the need for regeneration even as they understand the need for generation.

Certainly, first has come into manifestation that which is of the "earth, earthy" and then has come into manifestation the second man which is the "Lord from heaven."[6] As man has borne the image of the earthy, so must he now bear the image of the heavenly. But the weight of the burden of the Christ light, which is in reality no burden at all but only the powerful essence of freedom concentrated within the soul, must be accepted as the sole reality of life, as the reality of the Solar-El that makes man to understand, indeed, the meaning of the words "Ye are gods."[7] If, then, men belong to God and in the possessive sense are God's, belonging unto him, they also as his offspring must be sparks of the parent flame and thus not only belong unto God but also, in truth, themselves be Gods.

What a lie has been fostered down through the ages and slyly slipped into the religious patterns of the world. Men have then come to accept as truth, in the name of God, that they are vile and, in the words of Saint Paul, altogether "gone out of the way."[8] They do not understand how to "break the

Scriptures"; they do not understand that he was citing, as the Scriptures have cited from time immemorial, the negative patterns into which men have fallen. This is the ditch into which the blind lead the blind.[9] But those who have the power to see understand that energy must follow the thought and the thought must manifest the idea of its freedom here and now. For men to continue to wallow in the mire of despair or fear is a tormenting thing which denies the soul the power of the love of God.

The love of God infuses life! The love of God frees life! The love of God is inherent within life! It was the energy of that love that raised the Christ from the dead, set him on high, and ascended him into the heavens; and a cloud indeed hid him from the sight of mortal men.[10] "All, then, who follow me," he has said, "in the ritual of the ascension will be hid with Christ in God."[11]

The triunity of the spiritual experience forms a star of victory. There are three points in this triunity of the Divine, and there are three points in the triunity of the human. When all are welded together and the victory of the ascension is won, the star of victory shines in the firmament of that one's being and he becomes a victorious star in the heavens of God. In their messages of love, the stars in the firmament of God's being are telling all below, "Peace on earth, good will toward men. . . . For unto us a Saviour is born, which is Christ the Lord."[12] Christ is *Christos.* He is the light of the world and in him there is no darkness.[13] All who then dwell in this Spirit of the Christ become joint-heirs with him[14] of the ritual (the right-you-all) of the ascension.

How the Brotherhood at Luxor are chanting the Anthem of the Ascension! Hour after hour the rolling cadences and heavenly melodies pour upward as a white smoke, signifying a pillar of cloud by day and a pillar of fire by night,[15] telling all the meaning of these words: "Where I AM, there ye may be also."[16]

Lovingly, I remain

Serapis

3

The Triangle within the Circle

*U*nto You
Who Would Walk
in the Footsteps
of the Masters
Who Have
Transcended Karma
and Reincarnation—
the Scientists
of the Spirit
Teach the Law of
Self-Transcendence

As the fig tree puts forth her sign, so does the dawn of cosmic prescience in the divine aspirant manifest the signs of the Divine Appearing within the human monad. There are gusts of hope, laden with the balm of summer and the portent of good things to come, yet men must stabilize the consciousness during the time of testing.

The deviations from perfection occurred not in the flash of a moment but, in most cases, they were the result of a gradual weakening of character, less and less acceptance of responsibility, and the desire for mortal ease. Just as flabby muscles occur from a lack of exercise, so do the spiritual senses grow dim when the loud outcries of a maddening world are heeded; thus an unnatural imbalance of life takes place in the threefold flame of life's manifestation within each person so affected by mortal doings.

Men pay respect to science for they feel it has brought them "the good life." But without the scientist of the Spirit there would be no life whatsoever upon the planet and all would dwell in darkness or in the shadowed state of groping even for physical sensory perception. The lumens of the Spirit have softly caressed the darkness and pushed back the shadows as the will of God which is good has magnified his purposes for his created sons.

Men lament the pains and sufferings occasioned by their own karma. But what of those karmaless masters serving in hierarchy whose hopes are blighted again and again by unresponsive men? These are asked to stand as bulwarks against the hordes of mortal, shadowed substance and to intervene for and on behalf of mankind; whereas once men have received the little satiety of lesser purpose for which they crave, they sometimes quickly turn again from the light and immerse themselves in darkness as though their hopes lay within the turmoil of the world.

We ask ourselves at inner levels, "Is it because they doubt? And when they are convinced, is there no permanence to their conviction? Must they be reassured again and again as to the reality of the octaves of light?" What more shall I say than that God hath wrought the miracles of his perfection which are the momentary and eternal perceptions of the ascended masters' consciousness?

Ours is a forte of immortal rejoicing, and the trumpetings of our hopes echo even over the human sea. Men speak of Serapis with awe and reverence. They honor El Morya and the thrust of power. They "oo" and "ah" over the beauty of the consciousness of Paul the Venetian. But where are the legions of God upon earth, and where are the staunch ones applying to us today for initiation into the highest steps here at Luxor?

Returning again to the science of the Spirit, let me release knowledge whether or not there are any to hear, to appreciate, to appropriate, or to revere.

When men fail to progress it is always because there is imbalance in the threefold flame of life. The life that beats your hearts is a triad of motion, consisting of tripartite energies. The Holy Trinity of Father, Son, and Holy Spirit, of body, mind, and soul, of thesis, antithesis, and synthesis, of Brahma, Vishnu, and Shiva, of love, wisdom, and power, is also the pink, blue, and gold of divine consciousness.

The will of God is a predominant third of the whole, but lacking the wisdom of God, the golden illumination of his supreme knowledge, even power is stifled of action; and without love, power and wisdom become but the brittleness of self-preservation. The balance of the threefold flame creates a pattern of the ascension for all.

Dominant emotions are controlled by love and by the power of love in action. Because the wisdom of men is foolishness with God,[1] they perceive that not in the psychology of the world but in the balance of the energies of the heart do men bank the fires of the ascension against the day of their victory. The furnace of being, heated white-hot, must needs manifest the colors of the sacred fire and the coil from the serpent's nest rise upright, being lifted by wings of faith, hope, and accomplishment (faith, hope, and charity) until the Christ-man is enthroned in all. This is a scientific victory of the Spirit.

Not without precedent was this universe created. No idle experiment was behind the program but the ageless wisdom of the infinite Creator whose purposes are dimly perceived by men of lesser vision. Emotions controlled by love in balance with wisdom create a sharp etch of power which life cannot resist. Progress stems, then, from attunement with all of the triune aspects of God in perfect balance.

Blessed ones, if your tendency is to excessive study and the feeling of egoistic wisdom gleaned from the world's storehouse of knowledge, remember that with all thy getting, unless thou hast wisdom thy knowledge is but a tinkling bell or a clanging cymbal. And if the love which thou art manifesting is a love in expectation of return as a dowry from the beloved, thou art not cognizant of the will of the Great Giver whose every desire is to give the allness of himself unto the beloved. If thy power is as a flood or a raging fire which covers the mountains and the plains or consumes that which it seeks to benefit, thou must then master holy wisdom and holy love that thy power may be within the reins of the Trinity of Balance.

Classification is not so complicated as men imagine. The opinions of the mental body concerning the self, the overly protective aspects of the emotional body which often expends itself in beating the air as Don Quixote and his windmills,[2] the strenuous appeasement of human physicality as the satiation of every human desire and thirst is placed above the Spirit, the flagellation of the self by the memory body as self-condemnation mounts over a trifle—all take their toll of human happiness while defeating the divine purpose.

Men must summon the energies from the heart of God that teach them, by communion and friendship with the Divine One, how to govern the three and fourfold aspects of being until the seven bodies of man manifest the sevenfold plan of perfection according to the law of the square and the triangle. Then the cosmic circle of Life remains unbroken and the triangle within the circle becomes the symbol of personal victory. The circle can be placed within the square, and form then becomes comprehensible as a schoolroom of the Spirit and the place of consecration where the omnipotence, omniscience, and omnipresence of God becomes a reliable forte for the ascending soul.

Your consciousness is a priceless tapestry. Each day you weave upon it a motif of the Spirit, which is forever, or a jagged pattern which must be meticulously disengaged and rewoven as heaven intends. We are staunch and we remain the friend of all who earnestly, honestly seek to serve our cause and to find their freedom in allegiance to universal law which is universal love.

In the sense of divine commeasurement,
I remain

Serapis

4

*The Banner
of Humility*

Unto You
Who, Following Him,
Would Be Initiated
from the Beginning
of the Law of the One
unto the Ending of
the Mystery of Life:
Welcome to the
Disciplines of
Our Retreat

To embark on the path toward mastery, achievement, victory, and the ascension is an initiatic process. "Whom God loveth he chasteneth."[1] The few in ages past have walked through the gates whose narrow markings may not be too comfortable to those overstuffed with the vanities of the world.

It has been said, and well said, that no man can serve two masters.[2] Again and again we perceive a wanton disregard for spiritual law by those who consider themselves to be initiates upon the Path. Why do men choose to ignore the spiritual laws which gave birth to the universe and feel that they with impunity can completely escape from the law whereas their neighbors must come under the hammer thereof?

There is a dual mission involved in attainment. It is to be mindful of the great realms of Deity, hierarchy, and the friends of God as well as the octaves of delusion. Here vain men compete in the marketplaces for earthly prizes while the sands of time slip through their fingers, moment by moment, and eventuate in lost opportunities many times never regained during their allotted span.

Now we come to the stern business of accepting

those who have desired and asked for a dossier on the ascension that will give them the victorious patterns, stern though they may be, by which they may win their wings of light and attain to the stature of the immortals. We are well aware of the fact that individuals whose chief motivation is but an idle curiosity mingled with pseudointellectualism and carnal sophistication will, as dilettantes do, garble the most precious concepts and gingerly pick over those pearls of great price[3] which come to them as opportunity and are cast aside as that which "I already know."

Many desire to assess the spiritual stature of others, yet they have no median lines or markings upon the fabric of self which indicate that attainment by which they might at least suppose they could make a reasonable assessment. Imagination is their measuring stick, and the conversations of others their guideline. These often feel that they must lean upon the arm of flesh[4] and cannot tell the Real from the unreal because they yet lack that holy experience which they tell themselves they ought to seek.

I feel no need whatsoever to pamper the selfish, the greedy, the carnal minded. These have pampered themselves far beyond the fashion of ordinary men, and their dabblings in the realm of the spiritual will become an insult unto their own selves unless they achieve the greatest prize which a chela or seeker for God can have—humility. It has well been said, "God resisteth the proud, but giveth grace unto the humble."[5]

Therefore, as we begin to reveal to the students those cardinal virtues which are the very nature of God and are as compass points indicating the true path, we trust that souls in bondage to mortal convention will recognize that there is an octave of freedom and light, mystery, initiation, and manifest power which is above and beyond all the idle conceptions of men or the books that have been written on the masters of wisdom or the ascended masters.

Truth, beloved ones, is indeed stranger than fiction; and when men are willing to cast aside the ties which they themselves have made that have not brought them—no, not in an entire embodiment—the freedom for which they secretly long, they will understand that pride must go, or go before the fall.[6]

If pride goes, then the altar is swept clean for the gifts of divine humility. If pride remains, it doth indeed go before the fall of that individual into numerous pitfalls. These pitfalls are subtle, involving the character of the self. In order to outpicture in the world of form the intended God design, the individual must take up the crude block of roughhewn stone, cut out without hands, into which he has cast himself and, using the hands of spiritual idealism and the model of the divine image, he must seek to bring forth that holy sculpturing of identity which is identified with the Christ reality that, as the Word, went forth from the Universal Heart.

What is the value of reading our words and meditating upon them? The value and the benefit lie in the acceptance of the charge of light which we put into the words and behind them. These words, then, as glowing coals of holy truth from the altars of God, from the altars of initiation, and from our temple at Luxor, are trines of light intended to stimulate in men the knowledge of the holy symbols that reveal a goal-quality to man.

I recall full well when the Master Jesus came to Luxor as a very young man that he knelt in holy innocence before the Hierophant, refusing all honors that were offered him and asking to be initiated into the first grade of spiritual law and spiritual mystery. No sense of pride marred his visage—no sense of preeminence or false expectation, albeit he could have well expected the highest honors. He chose to take the low road of humility, knowing that it was reserved unto the joy of God to raise him up.

To raise an individual is a glorious thing when that individual lies prone in hope, in faith, and in charity, awaiting an act of God to reconsecrate the self to the simple quality of humility. For there is an act of false pride which manifests as false humility and causes individuals to appear humble whereas in reality they reek with pride. This false humility is often manifest in subtle ways and it is a mockery of the real.

Shun, then, all that is not real and virtuous, the thoughts of thine own heart, and mend the thoughts of thy heart if they seem to be trifling with eternal purpose. You came forth for one cause and one cause alone, and that is to manifest God's light. No greater purpose has come to anyone and no lesser purpose. While our mastery stands as a rainbow of promise to unascended men, this promise can never remain their guiding light unless they shed human pride.

Quite frankly, many individuals on the spiritual path use their contact with us as a means of attaching importance to their own egos. They but harm our cause; for the awful majesty of the divine light is able to probe men even to the depths of their very bones, and the flame of divine penetration that tests men before their ascension reveals the very naked recesses which are often unknown to individuals themselves.

I urge upon all, then, that they seek the banner of divine humility. If the masters and the Divine Presence of men through the mediatorship of the Christ have ever recognized any of the errors of men that have hindered them from becoming that which they long to become, they have recognized their pride. Pride takes many forms and true humility but one. True humility must be worn eternally. It is not a garment you place upon you for a moment, for a day, or a year, or when passing a test. It is an undergarment with which God himself is clothed, and unless it surround thee thy hopes of attainment are slim indeed.

In my present series of discourses on the ascension, I am determined to give in this dossier some of the disciplines which I measure according to your capacity to receive and your present need. Rest assured of this: all who will accept this teaching and bind it upon themselves as an act to do, an act of divine grace, will benefit immeasurably from it and from all that I am about to release as receptive hearts, like open flowers, become chalices of God's hope renewed in man.

Forward into the light, I say unto ye all!

I AM

Serapis

5

*Purification
of the Memory*

*Unto You
Whose Will
Is Harnessed
to the Absolute Desire
for Soul Purification —
I AM the Purifier
and the
Refiner's Fire*

And I saw the furnace of trials heated white-hot, and I perceived the testing of the matrices of Divine Love. I said unto God, O Lord, thou hast measured the Infinite by thine own strength, and thou hast placed the measure of the Infinite within man.

And as was spoken in Genesis, "Behold, the people is one, and they have all one language; and this they begin to do: and now nothing will be restrained from them, which they have imagined to do. Go to, let us go down, and there confound their language, that they may not understand one another's speech."[1]

Thus has the Cosmic Law acted and proscribed the borders of man's habitation to keep the way of the Tree of Life[2] and its fruit for the eating of those whose consciousness identifies with divine reality, happiness, bliss, purity, and those qualities that are native unto God.

Those who feel that the lure of the world is greater than the magnetism of the Divine ought soberly to consider the fact that all things were made by him[3] and that it is clearly recorded in Scripture, "Eye hath not seen, nor ear heard, neither have entered into the heart of man, the things which God hath prepared for them that love him."[4]

The mark of the beast must be perceived as the mark of a man,[5] but the tracings of the Divine are everywhere apparent. There are none so blind as those who will not see. Therefore, in searching for the ascension men must examine the motives of God. To do this properly, men must seek to enter the consciousness of God. There is a pulsating sound throughout the universe which has been described as the holy AUM or OM.[6] Others have referred to it as the Amen. It is the Infinite, moving through the cusp of the finite and quivering with the infinite life of the Eternal.

We come now to the place where memory must be cognized as the individualized *akasha* of a lifestream. Without memory, identity would fall. Without memory, purpose would not be perceived nor would there be any integration of purpose. The gift of memory is intended to be a purified faculty designed by God to enable men to rise in awareness, step by step, until self-mastery is gained.

Every ascended master has passed through the ascension flame here at Luxor; but long before the possibility of that event had any validity for them, they first passed their memory through the flame. The infestation of mortal thought and feeling, the variance from divine measurement, and the awful putrefaction of mortal ideas accompanied by greed, vengeance, egoism and the desire to expand the ego have wrought havoc with the tender folds of memory.

Not only are individuals themselves full of

dead men's bones and iniquities, as the Lord Christ spake long ago, not only are they full of hypocrisy, [7] fawning upon those who they feel will do them good and cursing by silence those whom they despise, but they are also forgetters of their promises. They remember that which they ought not to remember and they retain not that which they ought to remember.

I do not intend to spare those who desire their freedom; for unless they are aware of these things in which all men have engaged more or less to some relative degree, the necessary purifications cannot be accomplished which will enable them to enter, through the mediatorship of the living, loving Christ, into that God flame which is called the ascension flame and which acts to perform the final rite of absolution and purity, uniting man unto God.

Books have been written, courses have been given, and people have sat for hours at the feet of gurus; rituals have been performed, spiritual exercises, long readings, and meditations; but there is no substitute in any of these for the purification which the soul must willingly invoke and undergo. The "heat" of this "fire" is not always comfortable nor is it intended to be so, for even Saint Peter has said, "The elements shall melt with fervent heat"; [8] but the glory of the latter (the fires of purification and the results they afford) is not unworthy of the submission of the former (the elements of human creation) that bears the soul to its haven of eternal refuge.

Those who do not choose to take the instruction which I give may remain in the world and let the world be their guru. They may be taught by the harsh cadences of the world and beaten into submission for a purpose of lesser attainment than can come under our direct instruction. It is memory, then, I say to those of you who remain to listen, that must be purified not only of pride but also of all of the negative qualifications and habits of misqualification which it has absorbed through the centuries. Even in the dream state individuals are often thrust into the astral plane [9] unless they of necessity protect themselves, for there they frequently absorb the negative qualities of individuals who have no interest whatsoever in pursuing the divine path.

When I speak, then, of purification of the memory, I am referring to a memory purified to the uttermost, and the purification of the memory will be an awakening unto Christ identity and Godhood. Every lifestream has dwelled in the very bosom of the ascension flame before it ever descended, and this is why it was spoken by Saint Paul, "He that descended is the same also that ascended."[10]

The soul came forth with a thrust of purpose to do the will of God, and the human thought patterns which have been externalized have been an awesome blight upon the radiant patterns of the soul beneath. The human overlay has opaqued the light, and the travail of spiritual birth has yielded to birth in Matter and the misqualification of substance.

The contamination of substance upon memory has made it a frightening thing, an object of horror, whereas God would have it an object of celestial beauty where the Elysian fields can be perceived in their true reality and the world seen as but a figment of mortal illusion. When this occurs, when the flames of purification extend themselves into the memory body, it creates a spiritual magnet around the aura of the individual which draws him up into such Christ magnificence as he has never, even in his greatest moments of divine attunement, understood or envisioned.

I am urging upon you, then, the recognition of the need to purify your memory body of all the sordid details which are stored there, of all patterns whatsoever that are of negation, of all activities that are distinctly anti-Christ which may lie as obsession within the soul, and of all beneath the surface of consciousness which is not the purity of the supreme consciousness of the Christ mediatorship of your Higher Mental Body, or Holy Christ Self.

Some have sat before me at Luxor when I have given this very same lecture and they have said, "Send me back, for my consciousness is but a sewer of human reason and I am without hope." To these I have turned with a look of withering scorn and spoken these words: "You have disgraced divine purpose for centuries and now you stand at the doorway of freedom, this by divine grace. Would you return, then, to the turgid sea of human emotions and frustrations without receiving the benefit of our instruction when you stand nigh unto the portals of a complete escape?" Out of an entire class I have seen no more than one, then, turn back. And frequently, as that one has lingered near the portal, he has silently slipped back into his seat and gone on.

Do you see, precious ones, it is all a matter of perspective? Those who minister in the world to men's spiritual needs do so from the standpoint of pleasing men. We act solely from the standpoint of pleasing God. Our desire is to get the job done, to show men how to find their freedom.

Men require "spunk" and a straight spine. There is no question they have pampered themselves, and that with illusion. Straight talk and straight thought will do much to clear the way, and it will not place any individual outside the citadel of hope but wholly within it.

Men stay on the merry-go-round of human thought and feeling because they fear lest they fall off. But it will keep on going. So jump off the round of delusion and the mad whirl cf human confusion. Come to Luxor, to the place where I AM.

Lovingly I continue,

Serapis

6

The Awareness of Man's Union with God

Unto You
Who Would Understand
the Mission and the
Movement of the
God Flame upon Earth
I Say, Learn of Me
and My Contact
with the Fire of Contact
and Make It Your Own

Where is the dwelling place of the Most High God? This seeming mystery, answered by some as "God is everywhere," is not clear to the minds of many who seek their ascension. To the masses, many of the great cardinal principles of the cosmos are yet but a babble of voices with no tones that are clearly predominant.

Let us move aside the curtain and show the light behind the veil. First must come the concept of "hallowing space," then of desecration by misqualified energy. The idea that God is everywhere is perfectly correct, viewed from the standpoint that all things exist by his grace and life. If God is everywhere, then where is the mobility of his Spirit to move upon mankind and upon the creation which he has made?[1]

Gradation of concentration of consciousness, then, must be recognized; and it must be understood by the devotee that any point in space (that exists in self-conscious awareness and an awareness of the I AM Presence) may draw upon the very essence of the Godhead and cause the filaments of its awareness to glow with a greater measure of divine energy as that energy is invoked. Where the energy of God is consistently invoked

and the intervals of ordinary consciousness inter-
spersed between the concentration of divine energy
at a point in space are lessened, a greater transmutation occurs.

Let it be clear, then, that responsibility for
opening the door to divine manifestation is every
man's own. Just as men are responsible for taking
the pure stream of radiant energy which is their life
and misqualifying it with wrong thoughts against
others, whether they deem such misqualification
justifiable or not, so they are responsible for
opening that great door of cosmic opportunity in
fulfillment of the divine plan. This is accomplished
by drawing upon the creative Presence of God
released through His energies which are poured out
in the limitless emanations of Himself into the
world of the individual. These emanations are
known as the "fire of contact" that will consume
the dross of mortal thought and feeling and build,
according to the cosmic design, a complete sense of
victorious enfoldment by the Godhead.

One of the great teachings that was released at
Luxor when beloved Jesus attended our school of
ancient mystery was the unity of the Father and the
Son. The proclamation "I and my Father are one"[2]
has been heard and read by many who have never
entered into the meaning and experience of it.

To follow the Christ in the regeneration[3] is to
follow the light of the eternal Spirit of God in man
and to make of the living soul a continually
renewed creature. For it is the very nature of the
soul ever to transcend itself as veil after veil of
misqualification drops and reveals the transcen-
dent light streaming from out the very heart of the

eternal Father into the heart of the Son—that one who is the real you.

Individuals often have a sense of struggle about spiritual things just as they do about material things. To "let go" does not mean to let go of responsibility; it means to transfer one's personal sense of responsibility to God and then to cling to the vibratory emanations of the Godhead with the divine design held in mind. Too often students permit a sense of vacuum to occupy their minds in connection with letting go. To cease the sense of struggle does not mean that the divine effort itself will cease to work as an active principle within the soul and spirit of man—for his perfectionment as well as his enlightenment.

Precious ones, knowledge itself, when it is not used, can easily pass from the consciousness. When an individual understands that that which he has called "reality" is unreal whereas that which has seemed nebulous and afar is very nigh, he will be taking the first step toward the realization that God can, at any point in space—including the precise area of the individual's own present conscious existence—draw very nigh unto him and completely change his darkness into light. Jesus said, "If the light that is in thee be darkness, how great is that darkness!"[4] He was, of course, referring to the *misqualification* of the light that an individual at one time or another has received from God.

The consciousness of an atheist or an agnostic is in a category by itself. To deny or question the existence of the Deity may eventuate in the denial of the individual by the Deity, but the fact that man does exist and is aware of self and others is proof of his own present opportunity to receive the divine gifts and graces of God.

One of the problems, of course, inherent within present-day man is that he finds it difficult to believe in a God made in his own image—and rightly so. There is too much identifying by mankind of the Godhead with human foibles and human qualities. Even the human figure, the physical form of man, is often misconstrued with the Deity who is a Spirit. Simply because a Spirit can and does take form or ensoul it does not in any way render the power of the Spirit of less effect, nor does it give mankind the right to think that form itself has the power to control Spirit. The Spirit is the animating principle of life and it is intended to control the form.

Men must learn to bridle the destructive elements of human thought and feeling within themselves. As has been said, the well-intended have often led their unsuspecting fellows down the primrose path that seems to have the lure of mental greatness about it, and thus they reason away the blessed spiritual opportunities afforded them. Those of you who are preparing for your ascension or who are just getting used to the idea that this divine ritual is both a possibility and a necessity for men and women today should understand that nothing in the world is so effective in producing the proper attitudes toward the ascension in the light as the awareness of man's union with God.

Unfortunately, men cannot unite with that which they do not know or understand. Therefore, when one studies to show one's self approved unto God,[5] it is in order that the nature of the Godhead may come more clearly into focus in consciousness.

It is certain that happiness and peace are qualities of God. It is a further certainty that to produce vibrations in the world or even in the mind that are not conducive to happiness and peace is an offense against the purposes of the Deity. It is never a question that the Deity himself is offended by men to whom he seeks to impart only the highest gifts. Retribution comes rather from the impersonal Law that, seeking to bestow grace upon man, encounters the personal acts of men and finds it necessary that these acts be tossed to one side so that the pathway of the individual may be cleared of obstacles.

Men and women are often inclined to feel that divine justice is unjustifiable. The idea of a vengeful God is to them abhorrent. Let them understand that the laws of God are the laws of life and that it is death, or the opposing factors to the fullness of life and the abundant life, that is the enemy of man. ("The last enemy that shall be destroyed is death."[6]) The Great Cosmic Law then, in clearing away these obstacles, produces, because of the wrong acts of men, an act of retribution, or "vengeance," which belongs to the Law in the impersonal sense of divine adjustment and therefore "is mine, saith the Lord."[7] Without this clearing action of the Law, men could go on forever in a round of sense consciousness, vain competition, and destructive manifestation without ever bringing the self or this planet or any planet on any systems of worlds into the fullness of the divine design.

Inasmuch as the planet itself seeks to be raised

and to ascend, the victory of each individual contributes to the victory of the whole. Won't you please concentrate, for the sake of your fellowman as well as for yourself, upon producing in your world greater awareness of the Presence of God? It does not matter how close you may feel to him, the filament of being is capable of holding a greater glow of the Infinite. As long as you are unascended, there is room for improvement.

Ever upward!

Serapis

7

The Divine Right
of Every Man

Unto You
Who in your Striving
Would Know No Gain
but the Fruit
of God-Realization,
God Has Ordained
the Aegis and the
Guidance of the
Great Master Teachers

The concern of man for his immortal inheritance may not exceed the infinite concern of God nor equal it, but it is just and wholly possible that the concern of man within the relative sphere of his devotion can approximate the concern that every ascended master had prior to his ascension.

One of the principal problems involving the monadic consciousness is the insistence by individuals—when they allow themselves to come under the influences of the carnal mind[1]—that they use their own God-given free will to protect their individuality at all costs. Individualism is positively not correctly interpreted by the masses of mankind nor even by many among the spiritual seekers for greater truth. These confuse what we may term "human rights" with what we choose to call the "divine right" of every man.

It is true—and the world is proof of it—that human rights are being employed by mankind, and the mess of human pottage ladled out as enticement to the Esau consciousness continues to defraud the firstborn sons of their eternal inheritance.[2] But the divine right is another thing. The divine right is the immortal plan for universal man. The monadic intent—i.e., man's God-designed individuality and his natural gravitation toward the oneness of his True Self—is the first principle, or foundation stone, in which the inherent pattern of unique Christ-manifestation is self-contained.

Individuals seek without for that which is already within. Just as the entire pattern of nature is manifest in the seed, so in the divine seed the living Word is the inherent God identity, Christ identity, and soul identity of every man. This is what is truly meant by the statement "No man can serve two masters: for either he will hate the one, and love the other; or else he will hold to the one, and despise the other. Ye cannot serve God and mammon."[3]

The human master has attempted to enslave its own latent divine identity, which is the source of all life; and thus the human master has created a self-serfdom which holds individuals in bondage, not to their divine Presence nor even to the True Self, but to myriad world patterns whose end is always transition and change.

The changeless patterns of the divine identity are the best assurance to every lifestream that the course that man is running will be victoriously fulfilled. When the statement was made, "Eye hath not seen, nor ear heard, neither have entered into the heart of man, the things which God hath prepared for them that love him,"[4] it was intended to serve as a bond of understanding between God and man which would bring the blessed assurance of the divine intent into focus in the consciousness as a guard against the tendency of individuals to destroy themselves needlessly on the rocks and shoals of life.

In order to create that essential spiritual fabric between self-conscious Identity (that which clearly can accept the I AM THAT I AM as the True Self) and the universal Presence of Life, it is needful that the seeker understand to the fullest extent permissible under divine law the difference between the vacillating aspects of human life and those God-guided patterns which will render unto God those things which are God's.[5]

It is a great pity, in truth, that millions who seek for spiritual treasures do so out of the instinct of self-preservation, motivated by a desire to be good in hopes of a reward for so doing. Those who are motivated by divine love reach a place on the road that leads to God-identification where they recognize the supremacy of divine ideals as Abraham did, who heard the voice of God saying unto him, "I AM thy shield, and thy exceeding great reward."[6]

As long as individuals seek to master the world of illusion by themselves, they will lose their souls or be castaways from the kingdom that is not of this world.[7] Ever and anon, souls have sought to glorify outer-world conditions and to glorify themselves against the background of its facades; thus they have pursued a temporal crown right while they seemed to be pursuing the spiritual path. One of the problems today, and the principal one involving modern orthodoxy, is that while it is far better to have and to hold some form of religion than to have none at all, the concepts of mortal error about holy things are, to the present hour, very great and subtly concealed beneath a surface of apparent Godliness. This prompted Saint

Paul even in his day to declare of apostasy, "They have a *form* of godliness but deny the power thereof."[8]

Religion has become a cloak to be worn as a badge of merit in the eyes of one's fellowmen, whereas the seeker for truth and for contact with the hierarchy of light and the Great White Brotherhood must of necessity come directly under the aegis and guidance of the great master teachers. This God has ordained in order that all that is conveyed to mankind may strip the shard of error from their concepts about cosmic law. Then, through truth, progress can be made and the soul will reflect its pristine purity as motive after motive is transfigured through the absorption of the nature of Deity. Thus, rather than seeking humanly to qualify life with a spiritual pattern which seems to many to be a hurdle over which man cannot jump, he places himself in the arms of Divine Love and lets God unburden his soul.

God has never forced man to accept any spiritual exercise as a requirement for attainment, albeit these have been ordained by him and are available to the seeker that he might shorten the days of his earthly travail. God has indeed provided a beautiful link between reality and illusion through the concept of hierarchy and universal Christhood. As long as men and women think that only one man on earth could ever manifest the perfection of the divine plan, they will feel the lash of the law and perceive themselves as weak and ineffective manifestations steeped in the degradation of sin.

When sin is replaced by sincerity that recognizes the majesty of the Cosmic Creator, man will perceive with God that nothing that God has made could ever be aught else but good. And thus, inasmuch as man was made by God, man was created good. If there be any fall, then, from the goodness of God, it has been within the consciousness of mankind; and it is the consciousness that has fallen, then, that must rise until once again it unites itself with the goodness which was its natural origin and will for all time become its means of salvation to the uttermost.

Because the ascension in the light is the goal of all life upon earth, whether or not the individual parts are aware of it, it is essential that life should cognize that the fruit of striving is God-realization. There is no need to have a sense of struggle about this but only a sense of acceptance, which was stated by Saint Paul: "Believe on the Lord Jesus Christ, and thou shalt be saved";[9] which is to say, "Believe in the power of this Infinite/finite example as attainable by thyself, cast aside the sense of sin, sickness, and death, and enter into the beauty of wholeness (holiness) and Christ idealism."

If God so loved the only begotten Son, the Christ,[10] and if the Christ is the divine image, then this is the image of God in which all men are created. Hence this image *is* the divine right of every man. A return to this image need not be a complicated maneuver or a dogmatic charisma but it can become, through the simple consciousness of the Messiah, the means whereby all may enter the kingdom of heaven that is within.[11] So will thy consciousness become refined and ascendant toward the Deity into which all life must merge.

Progressively we move forward as little children into the kingdom.

I AM your brother,

Serapis

8

*Step by Step
the Way Is Won*

Unto you
Who Hold the Sense
of the Invisible Bond
of Hierarchy and
Who Would Grasp
the Meaning of the
"Thread of Contact"
I Say, Let the Soul
Be Restored to Its
Original Divine Image
That Its Eyes
May Be Opened

Now that we have viewed and reviewed the nature of God and man, we come to those disciplines and tests which precede the manifestation of the ascension currents by which men are literally raised into the God-domain from whence they came.

When the statement was made, "Study to shew thyself approved unto God,"[1] many heard it and apparently they accepted it. But the admonishment that was given unto John the Revelator (now the Ascended Master John the Beloved) when he asked for "the little book" must also be considered: "Take it, and eat it up; and it shall make thy belly bitter, but it shall be in thy mouth sweet as honey."[2] Thus of old was the declaration made to show the incongruity of the flesh and the Spirit and the necessity for the sweet acceptance by the flesh of the Spirit's burden (cosmic responsibility) and the manifestation of the living Word as the only cause for action.

Again and again individuals have been swayed far too much by outer circumstances. The weight of human opinion is also held to be of great import by many who profess to search for the kingdom but in reality seek the approbation and favor of men. If the eyes of men were opened and they possessed the quality of true perception, there would never be any question whatsoever as to what course they would take.

Countless examples of this truth exist in the holy Scriptures. There is the story of Balaam, the son of Beor, who was rebuked by the dumb ass speaking to him with a man's voice.[3] There is the account of the disciple Thomas, who said, "Except I shall see in his hands the print of the nails, and put my finger into the print of the nails, and thrust my hand into his side, I will not believe," and Jesus' answer to him, "Thomas, because thou hast seen me, thou hast believed: blessed are they that have not seen, and yet have believed."[4]

There exists in the world today a very dangerous sense of earthly sophistication which is wholly rooted in personal pride; in the grips of this pseudo-reality, individuals consider themselves qualified to be the arbiters of their own destiny. In the main, those who become muddled in this connection are those who have studied widely in various fields of religion and philosophy. It is as though men were convinced that by much studying they should enter into divine truth.

In order to study to show oneself approved unto God it is not necessary that individuals should become complete masters of human theology or comparative religion. In fact, it is often true that the more men study the less they know. And thus the words "Except ye become as a little child ye cannot enter in"[5] have great meaning when it comes to accepting the sweet sense of the invisible realities of God.

If I should choose from among the candidates for the ascension as to who would be the most apt to attain, I would always take the sweet childlike person who could accept divine truth with the light of joy in his eyes as opposed to the overly cautious, distrustful, and suspicious ones whose menacing countenances most often prove to be a threat to themselves.

You may wonder why I speak as I do. It is solely for the love of the Creator's own beloved sons whom I seek to resurrect through divine awareness into the great tides of cosmic grace. For these shall bear them upward and onward over all obstacles, sometimes at a dizzying pace and then again in the calm sense of knowing that holds the hand of God with the trust of a tiny child.

What child is this? Who is this Holy One? Who is this dedicated son who has the sense of the invisible bond of hierarchy? Let such a one grasp the meaning of the "thread of contact," as Morya calls it. For this "bond of hierarchy," this "thread of contact," denotes the fragility of the divine experience when man is yet identified with and wedded to mortal form and consciousness.

If men and women could enter into the etheric consciousness of God, the essence of the creation would be made known to them and there would be no need for the veil that presently exists in the temple of being between the Holy of Holies and the outer consciousness of man. Because the fashion of the times demands it, individuals seek to follow the styles and trends of mortal thought and feeling. What a fraud is mere existential "know nothingness" that seeks to raise itself up in the eyes of the universe and says of a life that is here today and gone tomorrow, "See me, I exist; and because I exist, I am."

There is a long trek across the parched deserts of self-testing and tribulation before the promised land of God-realization can be attained. The fires from on high must transmute and try the works of man [6] who seeks to become that which God already is and which God forever holds as the perfect plan for every man.

Why am I speaking thusly, beloved ones? Some say, "One minute Serapis blows hot and one minute he blows cold, and he tells me what I already know," while others say, "Never have I heard one speak as this man." All this vanity of conversation has no purpose but stems only from personal motivation and personal ignorance.

When Jesus said, "Father, forgive them; for they know not what they do," [7] he spake of the multitudes who passed through the wide gate. The narrow gate must exclude the paltry errors of men, but they must be willing to recognize the fact that they have erred and to come to that contriteness of heart whereby we can impart to them safely and in divine measure the commands of the Infinite over the finite mind and being. The psalm of David "The Lord is my shepherd; I shall not want. He maketh me to lie down in green pastures: he leadeth me beside the still waters. He restoreth my soul..." [8] shows clearly in its comforting vocalization that the soul must be *restored* to its original divine image.

Many men and women are not actually aware that the soul has been swept away from its eternal

moorings. They feel that the soul has been temporarily lost and that of necessity some thauma-
turgic process, spiritual formula, or doctrine of
salvation must be accepted and put to use by their
lifestreams in order that they might obtain their
eternal freedom.

They seek, therefore, for a religion with a
pattern that they can accept which will provide for
them, for all time to come, both forgiveness of sins
and the gift of divine grace. Men do not realize that
they themselves have lost their way and that it is
they who must therefore find it again. They do not
realize that their specific consciousness is involved
in this losing of the way and that the consciousness
which they have lost is the consciousness of the
Divine One which they must personally regain.

No litany or magical formula or even an
imploration to the Deity of itself possesses the
fullness of the power of realignment of the four
lower bodies in conjunction with the balancing
of the threefold flame. Realignment is attained
through the simplicity of the Cosmic Christ mind
that ever refuses to acknowledge that it has in any
way been involved in a state of consciousness
beneath the dignity of truth and the majesty of the
Godhead.

The sickening beat of clenched fists upon
human chests, intended as a manifestation of ab-
ject humility to the Deity and the invocation of
his mercy in time of trouble, where the true spirit
of repentance is lacking are of little effect in
producing the state of God consciousness and
divine awareness that the law requires. The true
internal sense of Cosmic Christ identification is

one of beauty and rejoicing. It is the beautiful acknowledgment and perception of the laws of love and mercy; it is the acknowledgment of the tender intent of the Deity to raise the soul up the cosmic ladder of creation. Step by step the way is won until each one beholds for himself the pure longing of the Spirit that seeks to become one with the created being which the Spirit has made.

There is no room for speculative theological argumentation in the Godhead, for God is not aware in his pure consciousness of man's frightening descent into mortal involvement. Only the Holy Christ Self has this awareness and acts to mediate, in his advisory capacity to the Godhead, the total world situation.

And so the present rebellion of the elementals against the impositions of mortal men continues, and the wails of those lost in the sophistry of false supremacy will continue even as heaven continues to beckon the sons of God onward, step by step, until through their attention on God their consciousness becomes the sole reality which the ascension flame is.

In freedom's name I remain

Serapis

9

*The Reawakening
of the
Divine Sense*

Of you Who Come
to Our Abode to Be
Disciplined of Life,
We Require
Purification of the
Muddied Stream
and Meritorious Deeds
That the Soul Might
Know the Holy Spirit
through His Gift
of Regeneration

Lonely millions fail utterly to see the link to God-reality that connects the finite with the Infinite and flashes forth meteorlike into their own souls to illumine the darkest night. The flow of God's consciousness, like an endless river, wends its way through man's numerous experiences which embody the sense of desolation as well as the thrill of exaltation.

When purification of the muddied stream of human thought occurs and the fount of his energies becomes a crystal one, reflecting light and cosmic energy which buoy up the four corners of the mind and so beautifully reveal to the soul consciousness the wonders of divine reality, the soul is indeed blessed.

Our disciplines are always for the purpose of regeneration, for without this gift and activity, which descends from the Holy Spirit, man could not attain to immortal life. Life is God, and he himself is the Tree of Life that stands in the midst of the Garden. Every manner of manifestation receives its life from him. Yet his masterful concepts as they appeared in the pristine universe, observed by man according to the immaculate concept, would quite naturally evoke from the heart the splendid cry "It is good!"

So simple and childlike are the attributes of the kingdom that men overlook them and thus they pass them by. The blessings of God are all around life everywhere. Life is replete even as it is complete with the most wonderful shadings of bliss which could be enjoyed by the Godhead himself; yet in men the power of perception—the sensitivity to perceive life itself—seems to be lacking. "Having eyes to see, they see not; having ears to hear, they hear not."[1] Neither do they sense nor touch the reality of God.

One of the greatest blessings that can ever come to an embodied individual is the reawakening of the divine sense and childlike wonder which so many had in manifestation very early in their lives. I would like to say in this connection that there are souls presently in embodiment upon earth in whom the karmic pattern of their lifestreams has been so utterly desolate and rebellious that even as babes they manifest a defiant and virulent hatred. While mankind may deplore the manifestations of these rebellious ones, it must be remembered as a mitigating point to all life upon earth that many of these individuals have been separated from the planet and from the life evolutions of the planet for countless generations, awaiting a dispensation of opportunity for reembodiment.

While it is true that there has been a certain definite action of punishment involved in their long separation, it is also true that they have been unable to work out any substantial measure of their karma while awaiting reembodiment. These souls, then, with all of their seething rebellion, resentment, and self-appointed misery, need a certain amount of understanding on the part of the devotees of truth that will afford them a measure of opportunity and an understanding of the goodness of the universe.

It has been said that whatever a man measures out will be meted unto him again, but it has also been said, "His mercy endureth for ever."[2] Therefore, while there will be plenty of opportunity in mundane life for these individuals to come face to face with the flood tides of rebellion which they have created and which they have made their dwelling place, it is up to all of us to understand and to grant them, even as a part of our own discipline, some measure of Christly mercy and grace. The savage energies which play upon these individuals must be warily watched, and those who work with them at any time should ever be alert to protect themselves by the power of light against the riptides of human aggression and shadowed energy which these individuals wield.

I have included this subject in my Dossier on the Ascension because one of the problems of spiritual discipline involved in winning the ascension is the tendency for individuals—after they have manifested a great deal of self-control through their contact with the ascended masters' disciplines—to become overly aloof and insensitive to mortal conditions which they must surely face until the last trump has sounded.[3]

We have seen numerous cases where individuals have performed all of the necessary rituals and spiritual disciplines which the law requires in order to merit the ascension in the light. Then through some unguarded treatment of an individual they have created a karmic pattern which has hindered the progress of their ascension for the balance of that entire embodiment, necessitating their return to the screen of life contrary to their own desires.

I wish, therefore, to point out that even an act of justified aloofness toward an individual can sometimes be a hindrance. Quite naturally you must be exceedingly careful not to permit your energies to become involved with any part of life in a wasteful or purposeless manner. But by a like token, if an individual seeks the milk of human kindness (which, when properly administered, is divine kindness), it would be well not to withhold it from him; for after all, it should always be borne in mind that we pattern after God and "his goodness endureth forever."[4]

Fear not what men may do unto you, but be the master of your own worlds by letting the God within hold high the standard of his love. When you give your loyalty to God, it does not mean that you despise anyone in his kingdom who may be manifesting a lesser understanding. The fact that individuals upon earth are occasionally disturbed by someone's adoration of a minor angel or cosmic being (minor, that is, in the consciousness of the observer) often provokes what you would call a "titter" in heaven. These objectors would not mind if Archangel Michael or Jesus were honored, but conceivably they find some fault because an individual might pray to Mother Mary or one of the "lesser" saints or even to an angel unknown by the masses.

I think heaven finds it a bit amusing that the laws of science are so highly honored by mankind and yet so poorly applied to spiritual things. Is not the whole the sum of all of its parts? And who can put his arms around all that is and embrace it? Is a grain of diamond dust any less a diamond than a ten-karat stone resting in the turban of a Mogul emperor? I cannot refrain, however, from commenting on the fact that by ignorance as well as deliberate misdirection, the mankind of earth today, in the main, are far from the beaten path of the spiritual devotee that leads to the narrow gate.[5]

Religion, intended to be an implementation leading to the soul's attainment, has become the means by which the enemy has blackened the consciousness of men and cast them into outer darkness.[6] In God's name, beloved ones, it requires more than just the wish to serve Him in order to do so, and it requires more than the wish to attain in order to attain! If you would be an instrument of God upon earth, you must stand tall and be willing to be counted as an adjuvant of God's cause upon earth. There are far too few who understand the mysteries of living truth that make men free from the delusions of the world.

I implore you on behalf of the hierarchy and in the interest of winning your own ascension in the light to look up to the realm of beauty and love, of harmony, security, and eternality, of joy, strength, and divine wonder—and live! There are many steps ahead.

Your teacher,

Serapis

10

Memory and
Residual Magnetism

Unto You Who Will
Remain with Me
to Be God-Taught I Say,
Watch and See How
We Shall Burn Up the Shroud
of Error and the Residual
Magnetism of Death by the
Living Consciousness of the
Ascension Flame

I would deal now with old residual magnetism. The law of gravity, beloved ones, keeps your bodies attached to the ground for a purpose; likewise, all of the components of natural law, wonderful as they are, are overflowing with infinite purpose.

The depth of the wisdom of God, when contemplated even in part, can evoke squeals of joy even as a small child, putting his feet into the cold water of a mountain stream, responds with happiness and delight. The law is most impersonal, blessed ones, as it expresses in nature. A part of nature is the faculty of memory. For example, thorns did not surround the rose in the early days of the earth. Certain destructive activity on the part of mankind resulted in the outpicturing by the tiny elementals of what men have called protective barbs; and thus long, sharp thorns were created as mankind's fears and doubts were etched on nature's memory and then lowered into the physical octave.

Religion, in the main, has supposed that God has created all things that are in existence; however, mankind have not taken into account the influence of their own thoughts and feelings in the acts of creation which occur daily within their own domain. Indeed man was given dominion over the whole earth,[1] but they have not reckoned with the concept of free will or with the longevity of the lifewaves who have inhabited the earth, supposing the span of the earth's existence as it correlates with history and civilization to cover a little bit more than five thousand years.

The many evolutions who have inhabited the earth have had ample time to change many of the outer conditions of nature and to bring forth from Universal Life many patterns which were never a part of the original creation. The race memory and the memory of nature is divided and subdivided again and again into such minutiae of manifestation as to put to shame the minds of the greatest scientists. We who see from the inner behold sublayer after sublayer of the creation that has not yet been split by the sharp blade of man's penetration.

There is the memory of the individual to consider, the memory of self—names, faces, places, concepts, recepts and precepts. But there is also another type of memory with which we are here concerned. Omar Khayyám wrote,

The Moving Finger writes; and, having writ,
Moves on: nor all your Piety nor Wit
   Shall lure it back to cancel half a Line,
Nor all your Tears wash out a Word of it.[2]

Of men's acts and thoughts this may be said: that they are all recorded, each one. Every subtle shade, every nuance of meaning, finds its way into the storehouse of the subconscious memory. These are literally interred with the bones of man, and they survive transition after transition; each time man reembodies they come with him again, composing his life record.

When the life-giving accuracy of this record is pondered for a moment and the effect of beautiful thoughts is considered with the heart, the need to rise to angelic levels of perception ought to occur to many. Why should men live in the dark, dank cellars of their human creation? Why should the subconscious knowledge that men have stored about themselves be tumbled out upon psychiatric couches? Is this what we may call therapeutics, or is it the putrefaction of old ideas disgorging themselves upon the consciousness of present-day man?

The panacea that men crave, if one can justly be said to exist, is within the domain of the same memory that holds the thoughts of negation; this the world has filled almost to capacity with the sordid nature of the carnal man. Now let them learn, if they would ascend, to eradicate this image by filling the folds of memory with the soft, gentle, beautiful ideas of the resurrection and resurrection's flame.

Nature has provided beautiful imagery, as environment, all over the world; and those who are perceptive to it can respond to it today in the very face of all human misqualification that has gone before. The greatest boons to the ascension are the immaculate concepts of God. His concepts about everything were benign and thus he said, by the power of the living Word, "All that I have made is good."

Consider, beloved ones, the meaning of discipline of thought that demands the immaculate concept about every part of life and refuses acceptance

of the patterns of error that as residual magnetism
cling to the consciousness of mankind as a shroud.
We shall see as we proceed—and I say this to those
who will remain with me to be God-taught—how
we shall burn this shroud and consume it to ashes.
We shall see how God shall transmute and change
carnal purpose into the splendid manifestation of
the living light of his Presence. We shall watch as
men and women today, in emulation of the Christ
majesty that rides forth to give a new sense of
victory to mankind, shall be born again, even
through the study and application of this dossier
that comes from the living, flaming consciousness
of the ascension flame.

We must be practical men when we deal with
these problems. We ourselves cannot possibly be
ostriches, even though our consciousness is in the
clouds of the immaculate glory of God. In order to
serve mankind, we must meet you at that level
where you are and point the way toward your
emancipation. The future is what you make it,
even as the present is what you made it. If you do
not like it, God has provided a way for you to
change it; and the way is through the acceptance of
the currents of the ascension flame.

Cause, effect, record, and memory of all that
is incomplete, of all that is darkness, and of all that
is intransigent must be willfully abandoned by the
soul who aspires to the freedom of the ascended
state. If you are content merely to wallow in epi-
sodes of your personal history, to seek for an intra-
psychic declaration of your past records, you can
have it by pursuing it diligently enough; but it will
be only a conglomeration of banal circumstances

from which, like a bad dream, you will one day seek to escape, or it will become an astral lure, as pretty trinkets and sparkling baubles, to distract you from the track that leads to your immortal freedom.

In order to ascend, you must abandon your past to God, knowing that he possesses the power, by his flame and identity, to change all that you have wrought of malintent and confusion into the beauty of the original design which, by the power of his love, did produce the fruit of eternal goodness. Cast aside illusion, then, veil after veil of the "personal person," and possess the willingness in the name of Almighty God to change your world! Thereby we shall be able to change the world into a place that will receive the masterful presence of the living Christ in a Second Coming of such dimension as to produce a race of Godly men, of God-fearing men, of God-loving men—of men who will build a pyramid of truth upon the plains of the world, which pyramid will stand the tests of erosion, of time, of mortal acidity, and of human nonsense!

The flame must not be lost. It must not be canceled. It must not go out. The flame must be upheld at all costs. And the flame is yours, for God made it so. God gave it to you, and it is yours to light the sphere of your identity that pulsates all around you, to push back the darkness until the glow of reality clears your world of fear, doubt, dishonor, and lack and provides you with everything that God intends his beloved Son to have.

Keep on, valiant ones. Lose not sight, for a minute, of the ultimate goal while keeping your hands upon the moldings of the present, for we shall prevail by unity with God and with one another. With strength itself we shall overcome, because God wills it so. Your ascension is God's desire for you.

In deepest love, I remain

Serapis

11

Doubt, Debris,
and
Deleterious Concepts

From the Heart
of the Great Pyramid of Life,
I Speak to You Who Have
an Ear to Hear:
By the Flame
of Your Own God-Reality,
Consume All of Your Doubts
of God and His Emissaries
Sent by Him to Save Your Soul,
Then Enter the Halls of Luxor
and Behold the Flaming Science
of the Ascension

Standing now at the portals of reality, we wish to dispose of one vicious human concept which has deposed many an individual from the throne of grace and has swerved more devotees from the path of righteousness than any could outwardly conceive. I refer here to the manifestation of mortal doubt concerning the reality of the ascended masters, the reality of the Great White Brotherhood, the reality of our outer endeavors, and even the reality of the individual seeker.

There is a doubt that is born of pride which causes individuals to shrink from anything which they at first deem to be unprovable. This doubt dispels faith, throws the consciousness into a state of trepidation, elongates confusion, and terminates the fruit of faith. No man wishes to be the victim of a hoax, and his personal pride tells him that unless he is wary he may very well be. Thus the sophistication of earthly reason overrides the great tangible realities of Almighty God which dwell in the invisible realm and are functional in all outer manifestation.

The wind blows and men see it not, but the manifestation of its effect is everywhere apparent. I do not presume that by a mere wave of my hand those who do not believe in my reality will suddenly be transformed into true believers. I choose solely to cite the law, to warn most sternly, and to reveal the treachery of this enemy of faith. Without faith it is impossible to please God; and therefore with faith and by his grace all things become possible, for "he is a rewarder of them that diligently seek him."[1]

It is lingering doubt that has lurked in the dark folds of human consciousness to become the seed of infection, spreading as a cancer throughout men's consciousness to their own destruction. Again and again doubt has robbed men of the birthright of their ascension and of all the divine happiness which the Father has desired to bestow.

In the name of common sense and reason, beloved seeker for truth, what is it that God has asked you to do? What is it that the ascended masters have asked you to do? Is it to tear yourselves away from the little games of life for a moment in order that you might view our thoughts and ideas? Is it to drown yourself in a sea of perdition or a gulf of confusion? I tell you, nay! It will always be your spirit of acceptance and your own nourishment of the seed of faith that will determine whether or not you can have the fruit of striving here and now as well as in the hereafter.

In reality there is no past nor future. There is only the present moment which elucidates from the hearts of the faithful the response of an uplifted chalice. It is God and God alone, through the hand of every ascended master, every angel, every chela of the light, and every soldier of the cross who desires to fill the chalice of your waiting consciousness with all of the gifts, graces, attunements, and measurements of a cosmic brotherhood of light beyond compare.

At times the Great White Brotherhood stands as a silent sentinel in the world of form, and yet the multitudes do sense the presence of this sentinel of the Most High God. Now and again they view it as an avenging angel that seeks to punish both church and state for those errors which are unthinkable in view of the nobility of life that has been made manifest in the true culture and progress of the world.

The present outpouring of vicious hatred between brothers the world around, manifesting as warfare and wanton murder, bears witness to the lack of influence which the major religions of the world have had upon the people. Men's motives and acts bear testimony to the fact that in all the times that have passed, that which has endured is the paltry manifestation of commercialization. Did not the Apostle Paul clearly state, "The love of money is the root of all evil"?[2] Behind the screen of the manifestations of war, then, are always the corruptible gains which men who cover themselves with the veil of sanctity often put forth in complete denial of the virtuous claims they make for themselves.

If the world does not soon awaken from its lethargy and communion with error, if it does not soon break through into the octaves of light and the realm of the ascended masters to perceive cosmic truth, the awful charades in which men now engage themselves will culminate in a holocaust of frightful destruction.

We are giving out our Dossier on the Ascension at this time in order that the faithful who receive it and transmit it to others may have the benefit of our thoughts, our feelings, and our release of the ascension flame into tangible manifestation.

We have much yet which we plan to convey of inestimable value to every seeker for self-unfoldment on the Path, but the debris must be swept away and the current problems disposed of. Men need not fear one another, for worldly men can but kill the body whereas the life of the soul is in the hands of God.[3] But we are, it is true, concerned with the life manifestations upon this planet and the opportunities that are being presented to them spiritually.

In every century the passing travails of the world have been most difficult for those who have been embroiled in them. But the way of escape to every man is the path of the ascension, and this is the gift of God to each one whether men realize it or not. The reason so few in every age have come to us here at Luxor in their spiritual bodies, as well as physically in some cases, is because the ritual of the ascension is the final initiation whereby an individual may earn his freedom from the bondage of the flesh. Freedom from the bondage of karma can come only when the law of cause and effect has been fully worked out. Jesus himself revealed this law when he said, "Heaven and earth shall pass away, but my words shall not pass away" and "neither a jot nor a tittle shall pass from the law until all has been fulfilled."[4]

I have had laid upon my heart, before I could further reveal the greater laws and mysteries of the ascension which this dossier is intended to convey, the almost brutal fact that I must dispose of some of the deleterious concepts of men before I can expect to give the full advantage of the current offering unto those who read. I urge, therefore, that all will pause to consider the motive behind my release. I want neither purse nor person. My only desire is that you should imbibe the nectar of the Divine One, transmute your difficulties, and find release from earthly bondage. I do not propose that men unascended should seek an escape from service but an escape only from those things that hold them in bondage so that when the trump of victory sounds for them it will be an ascendant victory.

There are many who have come close to the portals of the ascension who have been turned back by reason of some of the matters I have discussed in this and previous releases. Even the physical senses can be vehicles to the Divine; and therefore the keen and observant mind should never repudiate the existence of the Deity, of the soul, of the invisible Brotherhood, or of divine opportunity on the basis of either the reasoning intellect or the testimony of the senses. For it is all here. It surrounds the world. It is a swaddling garment of great light. The unperceptive see that which they wish to see while seeking to disprove, by hasty decisions, the glory of the ages that they do not yet dimly perceive.

I urge upon all the weight of cosmic consideration. Ponder the manifestations of life that are shown to you through the avenues of your physical and spiritual senses. Ponder whatever

God has given to you of glimpses of the Infinite. Realize that something cannot come forth from nothing and that Infinite Mind has created man in order that he should expand his consciousness toward the mark of the Infinite. The finite is but a leap across the chasm of a blind reality to the security of the domain of actualized proof. Men prove the law by doing the law. They see truth by becoming truth. They ascend by faith and not by doubt.

Out of the depths of the infinite wisdom of God and from the heart of the Pyramid of Life, I have spoken. Let him who has an ear to hear, hear.

Serapis

12

The Adaptability
of Man and Nature

The Penetrability
of the Sacred Fire of God

*S*tudents Who Would
Be Made Ready for
the Seraphic Hosts
Who Are Ready to
Become Teachers of Men:
Commune at Luxor with
Those Higher Intelligences
and Savants of God
and Enter the Very Fiery
Nature of God and of
the Divine Symmetry

The nature and identity of God is fire. "...Our God is a consuming fire."[1] The center of the minutest particle of substance is but an electronic ball of fire. Mankind have identified with the flesh; they have not understood the resurrection of consciousness from dead works. The concept of dead works implies that all that men do is a form of subservience to the transitory and carnal nature of man.[2]

The new and living way of the Spirit that involves the whole man here and now is calculated to bring about a transformation not only in the outer realm of flesh but also in the inward parts of the mind—of consciousness in particular—and an infusion of the vital energies of the Spirit. These have been deterred from manifestation because of the insulative barrier composed of mankind's dense electronic patterns whose absorptive qualities prevent the interpenetrating God flame from passing through the barriers of human thought and misqualified feeling and thus making contact with the God flame within the center of each cell, of each atom, and each electron.

We shall consider then for a moment the subject of cosmic penetrability. One of the qualities of nature which it is vital for men to understand is the quality of protective adaptability whereby nature, when challenged, provides through its myriad manifestations an immediate reaction, or "defense mechanism," on its own behalf. The interplay of these qualities of adaptability and their automatically instituted changes in form and lifewaves resulting therefrom, which continually impinge on man's thoughts and feelings, create many strange patterns in the consciousness of mankind that interfere with the original and pristine intentions of God.

The Garden of Paradise, when taken as an allegorical concept, presents another aspect of divine reality. That aspect is the quality of nature to produce at all times beauty, love, and perfection in all of its manifestations which stem from the original God design. Even a mutation, if it is guided by the intelligent spark of the Creator of all life, would endow form with an ascendancy rather than a deterioration factor. Therefore individuals must recognize that it is this same quality of adaptability in nature and in man which, when operating in reverse, builds defenses against the very progressive aspects of the original intent of God. Thus many times individuals do not ascend simply because they have created an inverse order throughout the natural manifestation of themselves, seeking self first and God last.

I think the domain of consciousness can be one of the most deterrent factors to mankind's progress when it is wrongly used. Consciousness is often the product of happenstance molded by environment, but it soon learns to override even its hereditary factors. As each succeeding generation creates a new fashion, retiring some of the old and preserving others of the traditional nature of man, the state of his consciousness becomes, in the main, most destructive because it pursues no cosmic constant but carefully yet haphazardly entertains a multitude of human fashions. The effect of this process upon the consciousness must be considered by the aspirant as he begins to denude himself of the sheaths of grayed mental and emotional substance which, like globs of protoplasm or the hard surface of an alligator, make difficult the penetration of the light.

Consciousness has its own strange forms of protection. The world is iconoclastic, yet it has a multitude of taboos and peevish traditions which it is not disposed to lay aside. Like a room filled with stuffed animals, the average individual who seeks for a renewal of consciousness has many "treasures" and "lingering mortal perceptions," carefully preserved in the storehouse of his memory body, which he finds difficult to cast aside. Suddenly to bring in the great God flame with all of its tremendous power would uproot not only the traditions but also the sanity and balance of individuality.

We prefer, then, that all who would make their ascension recognize the need for renovation, for a cleaning up of the body temple and a complete renewal and purification of the mind/consciousness. It is best, although it may seem to be a bit difficult, for individuals to decide that they will throw out *all* of their mortal traditions and pet concepts in order to prepare the way for the coming of the great God consciousness which is

able to renew the capacities of the soul and restore the active boundaries of the living temple
of God. ("Know ye not that ye are the temple
of God, and that the Spirit of God dwelleth in
you?"[3])

The idea of renewing consciousness is itself
causative in creating a desire on the part of
mankind to open the windows of the soul to the
original purity of the God design. Most men are
aware that their personal measurement is almost
totally that of a man. They also know that "flesh
and blood cannot inherit the kingdom of God";[4] yet
they know that the abundant life, the eternal life of
God, was bequeathed to every man as his immortal inheritance.

There is a tendency among men, which is
encouraged by the brothers of the shadow and the
sons of Belial who masquerade at times as angels of
light, to postpone the salvation of the soul to some
distant tomorrow or to the life hereafter. This
"mañana" which never comes is a furtive attempt
on the part of men to excuse their traditional sloth
that will not make the necessary adjustment here
and now in that era which God has intended them
to utilize for their own freedom.

As long as men are in a tunnel of mortal limitation, they cannot behold the valley of Shamballa
or the wondrous hills of Shangri-la. They must
first emerge from their own darkness and from the
cocoon of ignorance into the light of the spiritual
Sun behind the sun. The fires of God-regeneration
are actually manifestations of the triune nature of
God—of faith, hope, and charity; love, wisdom,
and power; even of body, soul, and mind. Yet

these similitudes including body, mind, and feelings must be purified—cause, effect, record, and memory.

Therefore we begin with the consciousness, and this renovation must admit the fire of the divine idea. The idea of the ascension must be considered as pertinent to the individual lifestream and not something designed wholly for another who may be more spiritually advanced or more capable of executing the will of God. Each soul must consider for himself the value of the love of God that gave the radiance of his only begotten Son unto the Manchild of his heart, in a very personal way.

I, Serapis, say to you, when the consciousness is imbued with the divine nature and that nature penetrates to the very base of that consciousness, it will, like a helium balloon, rise to the highest heavens of thought.

Now must come the penetrability of the divine fire into the emotions. The energy of joy and happiness, which is the great motor of life, must be engaged on behalf of one's self as a manifestation of the Christ consciousness. And last but not least, when mind and feeling have embraced the fire of God and the wondrous essence of his nature, the penetrability of that fire into the physical form—the brain, nerves, muscles, and organs—must come with a view to the elevation and the ascendancy of the whole consciousness. At this stage, healings and releases of tremendous spiritual power may occur to those whom you contact.

The use of the fire of the divine nature and the tangible fire of creation which removes the dross of human thought and feeling from the four lower bodies of man is a must; for if individuals will not consider in their consciousness the possibilities of that which God's life will *do* unto *them*, how can they receive the outbreathing of his ineffable love?

In our retreat at Luxor there are periods of meditation when for weeks on end just one of the divine ideas which I have given to you in this dossier is meditated upon consistently for hours and the full complement of its meaning is invoked from the heart of God. I propose, then, that all who receive these instructions shall consider them not as a release designed to be thought upon for a week but as a most precious treasure of our infinite intention for and on behalf of all who would find their way back unto the Father's Home.

Certain spiritual exercises will, in due course of time, develop within your own consciousness as you pursue this course of study to its fullest. After all, the specific exercises and instructions which we give are always derived from the very instruction which I am giving you here, for it is created in the similitude of that which we give at Luxor. There is a little difference, of course, in that instruction which we give at Luxor and that which we give through this spoken, printed medium; and that difference is primarily one of the timbre, or nature, of the students who come here directly.

Those who come to study at Luxor are already dedicated to the idea of mastering life and winning their ascension and freedom from mortal consciousness and form. They are not concerned with the trivialities and petty differences of life. They have already renounced the world and the things that are of the world. They come stripped of worldly yearnings and full of celestial hope concerning that which they expect us to do for them. They quickly learn otherwise and they begin to demonstrate for themselves, based on our instruction, the necessary steps of purification and preparation for the divine consummation when the soul itself enters into the consciousness of its Creator and the walk with God begins anew.

To those of you who can understand exactly what I am saying here and now I say, "Bravo!" for your souls will all the sooner attain the goal that we seek together (for we seek for you that which we ourselves have already received). A word of caution is now in order, for the instruction which shall come forth in the next few releases will be dictated from the highest seraphic levels. We urge upon all of you who receive this material to prize it with your hearts, your minds, and your beings.

Give gratitude to God for it, for it represents a vast and sweeping change in the initiatic system of the planet. It places in your hands some of the great treasures of the divine art which have been kept secret from the foundation of the world.[5] Yet the responsibility for its receipt rests with you. What you shall do with the material, how much value you shall derive from it, will depend a great deal, of course, upon your own willingness to forgo the questionable joy of seating yourself in the seat of the scornful[6] and, like a dilettante, selecting from the smorgasbord of the religions of the world those little tenets of faith that please you here and there.

Here you will be given a firm dictum, an

effective and tested release, a measure of divine grace incomprehensible to the untutored. Quite naturally, then, there will be a tendency on the part of those who are not fully aware of the intricacies of simplicity to disregard or override the holy treasures which we will make known to you, and we have already passed on to you a great deal more than the ordinary mind can with a glance comprehend.

Pursue this course wisely and well, then, for the seraphic creation of God stands ready to become teachers of men and, as in our temple here at Luxor, the rising stature of the unfolding soul shall be made plain to you. You will commune with those higher intelligences and savants of God, servants of the divine will who ministered unto Christ and minister to you today in the only way that Divine Love can, by reflecting the radiance of the very fiery nature of God which overthrows all trifles, baubles, pettiness, and confusion and brings in the stalwart nature of the divine symmetry.

God is your victory and your life. So we pause to honor him daily.

Your humble servant, I remain

Serapis

Faith in Divine Purpose

In the name of the beloved mighty victorious Presence of God, I AM in me, my very own beloved Holy Christ Self, Holy Christ Selves of all mankind, beloved Archangel Michael and Faith, beloved Lanello, the entire Spirit of the Great White Brotherhood and the World Mother, Elemental Life—Fire, Air, Water, and Earth! I decree:

O Archangel Michael, being of Faith,
Through my God Presence all doubt now erase
Open my eyes, my vision renew
Make of the many God's chosen few.

One by one we step through the door
Of greater faith than we've had before
Cast out our sin and our doubt in the Real
Help us to sense truth, God's Presence to feel.

I AM, I AM, I AM a friend of God
I AM, I AM, I AM uplifting his rod
Of implicit faith in my purpose divine
By thy blazing Reality now I do shine.

And in full faith I consciously accept this manifest, manifest, manifest! (3x) right here and now with full power, eternally sustained, all-powerfully active, ever expanding, and world enfolding until all are wholly ascended in the light and free!

Beloved I AM, beloved I AM, beloved I AM!

You are invited to procure your copy of *Heart, Head and Hand Decrees: Meditations, Mantras, Prayers and Decrees for the Expansion of the Threefold Flame within the Heart*, 36-page booklet, $3.25 ppd.; *Archangel Michael's Rosary for Armageddon*, 36-page booklet, $3.25 ppd.; *Angels*, 16-page booklet, $6.20 ppd.; and *The Science of the Spoken Word* paperback, $12.20 ppd. Ideal for your communion with God both in the Great Silence and in the science of the spoken Word. Make checks payable to and mail to: The Summit Lighthouse, Box 5000, Livingston, MT 59047-5000.

13

The Great Electronic Fire Rings

Seraphic Meditations

I

Unto You
Who Would Engage
Your Consciousness with
the Beings of Fire,
the Seraphic Hosts,
unto You Who Would Be
the Pure in Heart
and See God ~
I AM the LORD Thy God,
the LORD Thy God I AM

And I beheld the great electronic fire rings of the Central Sun.* I saw the surface thereof as of molten gold, blending with an azure blue. The sky became a sea and, behold, the soft glow as of pale pink roses of living flame bubbling upon the surface beneath, translucent and then transparent; a white-fire core that pulsed and rose and fell with a holy radiance inundated my soul. My eyes I sought to shield from the glorious wonder which I knew to be Reality, Infinity, and Love without end.

All Knowledge, all Power, all Love going on forever and having neither beginning nor ending were before me. And I saw the naturalness of home, of friends, of family, of all that ever was and is or is to come. Ribbons of interconnecting glory from this gigantic orb spread into space from galaxy to galaxy, from star system to star system, and the song of the music of the spheres moved upon the strings of my heart as a lute of fire. I heard the turning of the seemingly silent spheres and the tones of the cosmic fires, of dead and dying

*These meditations are spoken in the first person by the seraphim on behalf of the children of God—they are the observations which supposedly would be made by man if he were to attain the level of the seraphic consciousness. They are intended to be given in prayer form by all who aspire to these heights of glory.

worlds, blended with the nova, the eternally new, the children of space, interstellar systems moving outward into the far-flung deserts where the fractional margins spread apart, yet they were engulfed in the love of the Center.

My soul was separated from my body, and I understood that all that I had felt to be a tether of solidity and of identification with an integral, "dyed-in-the-wool" consciousness was no more. I roamed through spiral nebulae, through gossamer veils of light, through the flaming hair of the seraphim. I saw the places of the Sun and the turning of empty worlds as well as those that were overly populated with a progressive order of humanity.

I understood the message of the elder ones and I knew that the consciousness of a little child was the consciousness of the innocent of heart. I knew that the pure in heart should see God[1] and that the sophistications of the earth were a curse to my own reality. My heart burst as chunks of ice melted and became a warm liquid that revived all of the hope within my bones.

O Divine Love, thou wouldst not separate me—no, not for an instant—from the experiences of eternality. The last enemy that shall be destroyed is death. O death, where is thy sting? O grave, where is thy victory?[2] I know now no tethers to keep me from Thy Presence. Thy majesty with me is every man with me, and I with every man pursue the course that leads to Thee.

Consciousness can move. It can penetrate. It can fly. It can break tethers. It can loose itself from

the moorings of life and go out into the sea, the
briny deep where the salt tears of my joy are a
spume of hope, renewed again and again. I am
gladdened as never before, and there is no remem-
brance of the former conditions. These are put
aside as finite, as trite, as a passing fancy of the
mortal mind.

> Now I engage my consciousness
> With the beings of fire,
> With the seraphic hosts—
> Now I see God's desire
> To be the most intense,
> Glowing white radiance—
> A furnace white-hot
> Whose coolness is my delight.
>
> I see the shadows and the veils
> Of human thought and human foolishness
> Melt and evaporate,
> Vanish in the air;
> And all that I AM is everywhere
> And everywhere I AM.
>
> Consume in me the dross, O God,
> The impure substance of the sod,
> The dingy state of mortal fame—
> Consume it all, O Mighty Flame,
> And take me by the hand right now
> And lead me to thy light that glows.
>
> My soul as fairest, sweetest rose
> Emits the perfume of creative essence.
> Lo, I AM mine own God Presence—
> Taken from the flame of Truth,

My vital energies of youth,
My infinite strength is holy proof
That as thou art I, too, shall be—
Removed from all impurity
Until thy very face I see.

I AM the pure in heart,
For the pure in heart shall see God.
And as I join hands
With seraphic bands,
I know that out from the world of illusion,
Confusion, commercialization,
Unrealization, intense prudery,
And retreating fear of the light,
I AM come!

I have overcome fear and doubt.
I stand now clothed upon
With a garment spun of the Sun—
My flesh is clothed with an Electronic
Swaddling Garment:
It electrifies my entire form;
It renews my mind,
My identity with its original self,
And the glow of that Star
That is within me and on my forehead
Is one of hope for the ages.

I come under thy dominion
And all things come under my dominion.
I AM the Lord thy God,
The Lord thy God I AM—
For between the shores of our being
There is oneness,

The oneness of hope that does evoke
A release from all that is not real.

By thy grace, O God, I am made to feel
I am made to heal!
I am made to seal myself
And all that I am
Within a garment of electronic light
Whose impenetrability, bright radiance,
Shining down the dawn of foreverness,
Refuses acceptance
Of any mortal thought whatsoever
That limits my soul,
For by thy grace I am made whole.

Out of the light I am come
And with Thee I am unified to see
Shining down the century,
The corridor of years, of light
Of *pralaya,* of mantrams, prayers,
And ended human tantrums—
The celestial manifestation
Of God terrestrial
Raised unto the heaven world
Where the ascension currents,
As electronic essence,
Pursue in me every dark chasm
And intensification of mortal passion
Until they are milked—
Placed in the violet-fire caldrons—
And purified as substance of shining light.

O God, here am I, here I AM!
One with thee and One to command
Open the doorway of my consciousness

And let me demand as never before
My birthright to restore.
Thy prodigal son has come to thee [3]
And longs once again to walk with thee
Every step of the way Home.

So ends this section of the Seraphic Meditations made for and on behalf of those among mankind who yearn to find their way back to the arms of God.

Grateful I AM for the opportunity to serve,

Serapis

14

The Sea of Glass

Seraphic Meditations
II

Men of Good Will
Who Would Enter
into the Domain
of Creative Essence:
Experience in
the Coming of
the Flaming Seraphim
the Intense Need
for Purification
and the Magnificence
of Transmutation

And I saw the sea of glass, of molten white-fire substance cooled into light manifestation. And behold the crystalline beauty thereof spake of the need for purity. The purity of gold, of jasper, of chalcedony, of opal, and of every precious stone revealed to my eyes the magnificence of transmutation.[1]

How came the dark, dank smoke of millions of chimneys, black clouds filling the lungs of little children with the grit of sharp silica and magnesia? From whence came this rasping, this cough of desolation and the lethargy of men like molasses with the tenacity of glue? How came it into manifestation before us as impediments? How shall we extricate the beautiful soul from the stranglehold of delusory reason?* I gazed downward and then I gazed upward, and I saw the flaming seraphim coming; the need for purification within me was intense.

As an adjunct to their ascension in the light, men of good will must enter into the domain of creative essence, separate and apart from the

*This meditation, which contrasts the purity of God with mankind's abortion of the divine plan, is intended to show how mankind's misdeeds affect one another. Planned obsolescence and the measuring of the economic standards by the profit motive instead of the golden rule "I AM my brother's keeper" are major factors which have contributed to the retardation of spiritual progress on the planet.

individualistic consciousness. The recognition and affirmation that "I AM my brother's keeper"[2] as a natural outgrowth of divine love will enable all individuals who accept it to see that every human problem must be taken into account by the Great White Brotherhood and no situation or involvement can ever be considered as one's own business. On the other hand, embodied mankind by cosmic law are given rights which are protected even from the spiritual forces of the planet. Therefore, in order to invite the heavenly hosts to take an active part in assisting mankind, it is necessary that some part of life somewhere shall appeal to the ascended masters and invite them to help this planet in solving its many problems.[3]

Because it is the nature of God to assist his own creation in obtaining freedom from self-created bondage and every form of distortion that is hurled at mankind by the demoniac forces and sinister strategies of the brothers of the shadow, men must perceive that in descending unto the planet, as Christ did, and crying, as he did, "Lo, I AM come to do thy will, O God,"[4] one and all must without fail seek to alleviate the distress that manifests on a planetary scale. The road to the ascension is paved with many facets which require individual attention. Yet none of these facets must dominate or draw an unwanted amount of cosmic energy from the aspirant to the ascension.

We turn again to the seraphim:

"And I saw the maelstrom of human thought and feeling, the flashing of its colors, and the spewing forth of debris. Invective after invective were hurled against brother by brother. The awful struggle for deification of the ego, to raise the ego into prominence, was apparent. The seraphim came and they were as flaming streaks of fire passing through the atmosphere, and I knew that they possessed the quality of cosmic penetrability; like cosmic rays they could pass through the flesh form of man, through his thoughts and feelings. When penetration occurred and the seraphim flew through human consciousness, what residue was left behind or what absorption was accomplished?

"I saw clearly that absorption was accomplished and that residue was left behind—absorption by reason of instantaneous transmutation of all substance that came nigh unto their trajectory. I noted also that the residue left behind was of intense white-fire devotion, charged with a yearning for purity. I perceived that this quality lingered within the consciousness of many; and yet, unless it was fed or accepted by them, its decay rate in their consciousness would be of relatively short term, for a disassociation of these ideas would cause the lingering sparks of the seraphim to pursue the parent body and leave their temporarily unwelcome home."

I trust, then, that the chelas of light, whose hopes rest in God and in the power of the ascension, who are mindful of the intercession of the angelic hosts and who recognize that the angelic hosts can and do enter into their consciousness, will also understand that affinitizing with the angelic consciousness—that is, with the consciousness of the seraphim—is tantamount to retaining the benefits of the seraphic hosts.

I know of no power more valiantly capable of

assisting anyone into his own ascension in the light than the transmutative efforts toward Cosmic Christ purity which are emitted by the seraphic hosts. In our retreat at Luxor, the meditations upon the seraphim are a very important part of our spiritual instruction. Jesus himself spent a great deal of time in communion with the seraphic hosts. This developed in him the superior power whereby he could cast out demons and take dominion over the outer world of form.

I am fully aware of the fact that the intensely involved and deep instruction appearing between the lines of this release and others may cause some distress to those who do not fully grasp its principles. Be not concerned, beloved children, seekers for the light. Did you expect when you began to search for God that you would find him without mystery? Did you expect that a study in Truth that is progressive would be without involvement, without commitment, and without the need for responsible action? Understand, then, as I give this Dossier on the Ascension that its sole purpose is the raising up of God-magnificence in the consciousness of those who read and understand.

We are compelled, then, by cosmic law to give you those techniques and points of the law that are best designed to consummate in you a burning desire for spiritual progress that "will not take no for an answer!" In heaven's name, blessed ones, you cannot expect to move forward into the light by following the same old familiar ways of the flesh and the mortal mind which you have long known. If new ways of thought and feeling are to be made, they must be produced at times by a shattering and abrupt departure from the old.

The disciplines of the ascension require your unswerving devotion and your utmost attention. You cannot produce the necessary changes in consciousness that will fit you for our cosmic band unless there is a willingness on your part to relinquish ties to human foolishness. Vanity is always indicative of vain effort. Conversely, those who invest their energies, securing for themselves a position of spiritual triumph whereby their victory can significantly assist the evolutions of the planet, will be filling a needed manifestation for and on behalf of the original God design.

If man was created by God, then that Goodness which is the nature of God should and ought to manifest in consciousness, not just according to someone's opinion, but according to the original plan. There is more science in this dossier than any among mankind will be able to perceive by a casual reading. The science we have placed here is calculated to perform an act of great blessing to those who read in order that they may truly understand.[5]

In the steadfastness of cosmic progress
I remain

Serapis

15

The Predication of God

Seraphic Meditations
III

Little Children
Who Would
Enter into the Place
of the Son of God,
the Consciousness
Where God Is:
I AM and Because
I AM You Are,
We Are, They Are —
It Is. Therefore Enter
Thou the Open Door
of Paradise to Come

Concluding the Seraphic Meditations prior to a higher step in our dossier, we release the thoughts of the Captain of the Seraphic Bands, Justinius:

I beheld the predication of God, the First Cause, unsullied, magnificent in brightness, qualifying each monadic release with the intensely glowing similitude of the Divine. What a delight of sameness, defrauding none; jealousy was unborn. But the fire remained not tiny and not finite. It was a growing spiral of concept. From the dot, the circles emerged and, as the hands of a clock, spun a cone in space that, like a golden ladder, scaled the heights, probed the depths, and unified the diverse.

Where is division, then, among us? It is not. All that divides is not among us. All that seeks to conquer is not among us, for we are enamored by His love. And the blush of a flower petal is translucent unto us, for His light streams through the substance as a window lattice of exquisitry.

Naturally endowed and endowing nature, thy omnidirectional rays flood forth translucent superiority—transparency—revealing as translucency, concealing and variegating the motif of a child's eye delight. I AM and because I AM you

are, we are, they are—It is. All comes into focus as
a thrilling, throbbing unity of purpose at work—
action with no room for reaction, for all is auto-
mated to express individuality, purpose, action,
heartbeat, unity, fire of purpose, and continuity.
Continuity and immortality are one, and all that
endures is of worth; and all that is of worth endures to repair its highest glory behind the veils of
ever-receding transcendency.

No ultimate save ultimate purpose. No end
save new beginnings. No frustration but never-
ending revelation. Youth and newness, friendships
and light expansion as God's vision beholds manifestation, as manifestation by God's vision expands
vision as an adjunct to creative re-creation. And
limitation is perceived as imitation, schooling the
manifestation within the microcosmic domain until, by reason of soul advancement, the imitator
becomes the limitless Imitator. The soul is raised to
higher dimensions of service as God goes into action to graduate the lesser manifestation of himself to complete the glory of his plan.

"Verily I say unto you, Except ye be converted
and become as little children, ye shall not enter
into the kingdom of heaven."[1] The surreptitious
consciousness of man, like an ink cloud or the
spew of a giant squid, opaques the atmosphere of
reality and holds man submerged. Now we break
the bonds with all of their tenacity, and we feel the
magnetism of the world being exchanged for the
magnetism of heaven.

Liberty is born in the soul—
No more will man be satisfied with lesser goal.

The baubles and trinkets of the world
Have their place,
But the place of the Son of God
Is the consciousness where God is.

The place where God is not
Or where lesser images of him hang
As useless icons upon the walls—
This no longer holds the soul
Which seeks to fly the realm of mortal delusion
And neath the canopy of Good Will
See and entertain the reality of the angels,
Of the ascended masters,
Of that cloud-capped realm
Where the soul, with childlike laughter,
As a bubbling stream
Moving toward the Sea of Identity,
Feels the freedom of the wind
And the power to stir the zithers
Of lesser consciousness
With a sense of beauty and of the subtlety
That hangs like a brilliant bubble
Whose watery, airy veil
Drapes the transparency of mirrored iridescence
To the waiting eye.

The realm of angels is not without delight
And ascended master reality awaits the flight
Of souls who yearn to break the bonds
Of hopelessness that defraud the world situation
From the wonders of God's radiant intent—
Captured so penuriously
Within the fabric of ritual, prayers, and dogma
But held so beautifully
As pulsing flame of threefold God-delight—

Love, wisdom, and power
Within the heart and soul.

And now as I await the expansion
Of the great Macrocosmic world
Within the microcosmic realm of self,
I see that born in me
Is the power of limitless expansion every hour.
O God, I thank thee for the shining hours
That come composed of minutiae
Of minutes, seconds, and of micropause,
While mind does turn to record forever
Thy immortal laws.

What is this pearly door before which I stand?
Is this some realm of dream
Where lurks a shadow band?
Nay, for that face I see so clearly now,
Peeping out from behind the open door,
Is an angel face
That I have known in long ago before.
My thoughts slid down the finite spout
And all the light of hope went out—
The rope I broke
And fear of icy desolation seized me round
Till I was then completely bound
In all delusions' cords and vanities.

Now once again I rise,
Pulsation toward the skies
Where God and home as fires of love do glow,
Renewing courses raised to sources
All divine.

My soul begins again to climb
The stairway ladder where

Each meaning comes
So tender, sweet, and pure—
It makes me to know
That God's own plan secure
Will hold me when the world
Seems nigh to fall apart.

For after all there is but one great Heart
Which beats our own,
And we must rise to fairer realms
Where we atone,
At-one with all that really lives,
For paradise is Life that gives
Nobility of efforts just
To counteract the concept of the dust
From which God did make in hope
A living soul—
And through the fragrant mists
Reveals the goal
Of paradise to come.

Yours in the name of the magnificent God flame,
the Captain of the Seraphic Hosts,

Justinius

I trust you have enjoyed this release and
conclusion of our meditations with the seraphim.
Next week we begin a vital journey into the Infinite.

By his grace I AM

Serapis

16

The Great God-Emanation
of Life within You

*For the Student
Who Would Be in Rapport
with the Teacher
and Thereby Secure
a Portion of the Teacher's
Progressive Advancement:
Now Is the Time
When You Must Turn
the Great Will-Key
in the Door of
Cosmic Opportunity*

To be in rapport with the Teacher is to secure a portion of the Teacher's progressive advancement. Even an ordinary schoolteacher knows that a daydreaming child or one whose attention wanders will not absorb as well as those who are attentive. Some have carelessly read our instruction on the ascension. Others have sincerely and with diligence sought to understand all that they could. Some have bypassed our words as though they emanated from an ordinary human source.

I wish to emphasize that many souls have journeyed on the path toward God under the most strenuous conditions and through the road of tears and travail in order to come and hear a less formalized instruction than that which I have offered so freely to all. Now as we come to the point where I shall impart unto you the lesser and greater mysteries of the ascension, I wish to disengage my energies completely from the personal level. In order to do this may I remind each student that all that I have given before—that is, this total instruction—is knowledge for which you individually will be held accountable. Those who have not read it at all but to whom it has been sent also have a very definite responsibility. Those who have read it casually without understanding have an equal responsibility.

Inasmuch as this offering of the ascended masters is joyously and lovingly given, it ought to follow that those who receive it should likewise do so in love and grace. I say this in departing from my personal contact with you that I may identify totally with the great God-emanation of Life that is within you and that is the source of all of the Life you have been given.

It is essential that your mind should not wander, that your consciousness should not waver, that you should not engage your attention in lesser things during the time that you have set aside to seek to understand these greater things. In God's name, beloved ones, if the instruction on the ascension were so simple, which in one sense it is, and so easily mastered, which it also is, why is it that in every generation so few are able to win this precious gift of God that is intended for all people?

According to the Karmic Board, the fault lies neither with the instruction nor with the Teacher. If the fault lies with neither Teacher nor instruction, where does it lie? Strictly at the doorstep of the average individual who is so serious about trite and trivial things which seem of great moment to him that he scarcely realizes how very important the invisible glory of the kingdom of God is. This invisible glory, which is brought to you weekly as the tangible offering of the ascended masters, is the most serious and gracious gift of Life that man could ever have—aside from the original momentums of his Great God Self which lie dormant within every son of God.

These momentums of personal glory await the kiss of the "Prince of the Realm"[1] who will bring the "Sleeping Beauty" of the Divine Self into manifestation and quicken in you every good thing in order that all that has been dormant and inactive may be safely raised up in the service of the King (the mighty I AM Presence) for your own freedom's sake.

I thank you for such attention as you have given and for that capacity of divine service which you have offered. We can ask no more, nor do we. Your Divine Presence will always be the illuminator of the self, and the lesser light can but reflect the greater light. It behooves each individual, then, to understand the great part that the conscious will must play in the release of the self from all outer circumstances into the glories of the immortal kingdom.

The drill which we give in words may seem repetitious to the outer mind, but it is absolutely needed in order to counteract the tremendously repetitive and definitely luring attractions of the outer world which seek to engulf man and his total energies into a waste of Cycle's opportunity. Men flit from this to that and from that to this. They struggle everywhere to find some solace to a wounded egoistic consciousness. Their basic insecurities are legion, and they know not which way to turn. The way of the Divine is the only way that leads Home. All other doors and avenues are blind alleys for which each lifestream must one day give account.

Sweet surrender to the Presence of God is initiated first of all in the will. The will is the key whereby the human self has its say.[2] You have willed lesser images. You have willed imperfection. You have willed subservience to others and to the world order. You have closed your eyes to the truths of God that stand glaringly apparent, even to a child. You have owned and allowed that there is more to life than meets the eye, admitting an infinite yet an unknown purpose.

The schemes of men are all in vain.
The tracks are there, but where's the train?
Men say, "Choo, choo"
But choose not right—
They backward go, away from light,
And chug along in sense immersion
While seeing not Life's great dispersion—
Energies, like centipedes
A-stealing time and Godly needs
From men and women God has made
To be both courageous and unafraid—
To stand up and be counted, then,
To master all that should not have been
And in a state of one accord
To learn in truth to love the Lord—

Now comes the time when the great will-key
Must be turned in the door of cosmic opportunity;
Now comes the time when the old
Must be renewed,
When all that is invisible
Must once again be reviewed.
For God is one,
His flame is love—
He longs to raise man up above
Where gazing downward he can see

The beauteous pathway of the free,
Wending from the plains below—
God's life is always on the go.

Through men he flows his wisdom wise,
The power to see and televise
The joys of heaven to all men,
Seek cosmic leaven once again,
And raise the loaf of Eucharist
By keeping always sacred tryst,
A vigil of Communion flame
That keeps the faith in God's own name.

His honor is untarnished light,
'Twill 'luminate the darkest night
And make each hour a shining one
Where Victory's light from Cosmic Sun
Can raise a banner for everyone.
O Peace on Earth, Good Will to Men,[3]
Begin in me and in all men
To rend the veil between the night
And the beauty of the light,
To set me loose from all that binds,
Remove the blinders from my mind,
And let me now and ever be
Enamored by thy love for me.

I AM thy son, O Lord divine,
I stand before ascension's beams—
Thy flame will make me ever climb
On the ladder of our God;
I joy to walk beneath his rod
And by instruction of his Word
To wield the power of his sword.
A truth that can only be adored

Will speak to hearts the world around
About the Peace I now have found
And see that clouds of glory will
Surround me now, my cup to fill.

O Peace, be still[4] and let thy joy
Flood through my heart,
As of thyself thou dost impart
A greater measure of thy power
To mould my victory every hour
And help me when the going's tough
To know that God does never bluff
But keeps his Word "I AM IN ALL"
To be an answer for each call.

O come, beloved Holy One,
By flames of great ascension's sun
And weave the garment of thy flame
Around this temple in God's name—
A wedding garment for thy feast[5]
When strife is ended, war shall cease;
The wall is down, the way is plain—
I rise—I nearer draw
By Christ obedience to thy law.

Serapis

THE CHART OF YOUR DIVINE SELF

The Chart of Your Divine Self

There are three figures represented in the Chart of Your Divine Self. We refer to them as the upper figure, the middle figure and the lower figure. These three correspond to the Christian Trinity: The upper corresponds to the Father, who is one with the Mother, the middle to the Son, and the lower to the temple of the Holy Spirit.

We address our Father-Mother God as the I AM Presence. This is the I AM THAT I AM, whom God revealed to Moses and individualized for every son and daughter of God. Your I AM Presence is surrounded by seven concentric spheres of rainbow light. These make up your Causal Body, the biding place of your I AM Presence. The spheres of your Causal Body are successive planes of God's consciousness that make up your heaven-world. They are the "many mansions" of your Father's house, where you lay up your "treasures in heaven." Your treasures are your words and works worthy of your Creator, constructive thoughts and feelings, your victories for the right, and the virtues you have embodied to the glory of God.

The middle figure in the Chart is the only begotten Son of the Father, the Light-emanation of God, the Universal Christ. He is your personal Mediator and your soul's Advocate before God. He is your Higher Self, whom you appropriately address as your beloved Holy Christ Self. John spoke of this individualized presence of the Son of God as "the true Light, which lighteth every man that cometh into the world." He is your Inner Teacher, your Divine Spouse, your dearest Friend and is most often recognized as the Guardian Angel. He overshadows you every hour of the day and night.

The lower figure in the Chart is a representation of yourself as a disciple on the path of reunion with God. It is your soul evolving through the planes of Matter using the vehicles of the four lower bodies to balance karma and fulfill her divine plan. The four lower bodies are the etheric, or memory, body; the mental body; the desire, or emotional, body; and the physical body. The lower figure is surrounded by a tube of light, which is projected from the heart of the I AM Presence in answer to your call. It is a cylinder of white light that sustains a forcefield of protection 24 hours a day, so long as you maintain your harmony in thought, feeling, word and deed.

Sealed in the secret chamber of your heart is the threefold flame of Life. It is your divine spark, the gift of life, consciousness and free will from your beloved I AM Presence. Through the Love, Wisdom and Power of the Godhead anchored in your threefold flame, your soul can fulfill her reason for being on earth. Also called the Christ flame, the threefold flame is the spark of the soul's Divinity, her potential for Christhood.

The silver (or crystal) cord is the stream of life, or "lifestream," that descends from the heart of the I AM Presence to the Holy Christ Self to nourish and sustain the soul and her four lower bodies. It is over this 'umbilical' cord that the light of the Presence flows, entering the being of man at the crown chakra and giving impetus for the pulsation of the threefold flame in the secret chamber of the heart.

The lower figure represents the son of man or child of the Light evolving beneath his own Tree of Life. The soul and the four lower bodies are intended to be the temple of the Holy Spirit. The violet flame of the Holy Spirit envelops the soul as it purifies. The Chart of Your Divine Self shows how you should visualize yourself standing in the violet flame. You can invoke the violet flame daily in the name of your I AM Presence and Holy Christ Self to purify your four lower bodies in preparation for the ritual of the alchemical marriage — your soul's union with the Beloved, your Holy Christ Self.

Shown just above the head of the Christ is the dove of the Holy Spirit descending in the benediction of the Father-Mother God. When your soul has achieved the alchemical marriage, she is ready for the baptism of the Holy Spirit. And she may hear the Father-Mother God pronounce the approbation: "This is my beloved Son in whom I AM well pleased."

When your soul concludes a lifetime on earth, she gravitates to the highest level of consciousness to which she has attained in all of her past incarnations. Between embodiments she is schooled in the etheric retreats until her final incarnation, when the great law decrees she shall return to the Great God Source to go out no more.

Your soul is the nonpermanent aspect of your being, which you make permanent through the ascension process. By this process your soul balances her karma, bonds to your Holy Christ Self, fulfills her divine plan and returns at last to the living Presence of the I AM THAT I AM. Thus the cycles of her going out into the Matter Cosmos are completed. In attaining union with God she has become the Incorruptible One, a permanent atom in the Body of God. The Chart of Your Divine Self is therefore a diagram of yourself — past, present and future.

Further instruction on the Chart of Your Divine Self is given in *The Lost Teachings of Jesus Book 2, Climb the Highest Mountain* and *The Astrology of the Four Horsemen* by Mark L. Prophet and Elizabeth Clare Prophet.

17

The Great Deathless Solar Body

O Thou Mortal
Who Wouldst Put On
Thy Garments of Immortality,
O Thou Son Who Wouldst
Return to the Father:
Call Thou upon Thy God
to Commence the Weaving of
Thy Deathless Solar Body
Spun Out of the Light
of the Sun

The parable of the wedding garment is indicative of the great Deathless Solar Body which man must weave.[1] The anchor of man's identity which he must willingly cast beyond the veil is symbolical of this wedding garment. Just as your tube of light is woven of the great redundant God energies which answer every call, just as the violet flame pulses through all who call upon the name of the Lord and visualize this beautiful flame, so does God answer the call of man to commence the weaving of his Deathless Solar Body.

This body of light is begun in the heart of your God Presence and it is spun out of the light of the sun of that Presence as man below consciously invokes the holy energies of God. These are sent to him (where they are focused in the threefold flame within the heart) and then raised back through the top of his head up the silver cord into the hands of his Holy Christ Self for transmittal to the heart of the Presence where the garment is gradually woven as the wedding garment of the Lord.[2]

In order to comprehend the meaning of the ascension flame, men must understand the meaning of the Deathless Solar Body as well as the meaning of the possibilities of their own ascension.

Only the purified energies of their hearts can be returned to the heart of the Presence so that God may actually create a garment of pure light with which the aspiring soul may be clothed. Therefore only those energies of the Presence which are retained by man in purity and in love are a worthy offering which may be returned to God for the preservation of man's immortality.

This garment of light possesses the power of levitation but it also possesses conformity to the outer and Inner Self. It conforms to the Inner Self because it is spun from the energies of God and the original pristine pattern of God for each lifestream. Embodying within itself, therefore, the principles of victory, it holds with the Presence and with all God-magnificence; possessing also conformity to the human, it is able to conform to the highest in man of the divine nature which he has externalized in the world of form, and it finds an anchor point in the human octave through all of the qualities and character of man which are congruent with the Divine.

Men find, however, that for the most part their behavior patterns are the result of selfish human activity whereby they regard their human rights as so sovereign that they conclude they are incapable of doing wrong as long as their actions remain within the bounds of these so-called rights. This is just as dangerous as the notion that they are incapable of doing right, which is equally treacherous. The correct attitude is to be found in the distinct realization that, when called upon, God can act in man and that all that God does in man will be according to His plan.

If men's lives are lived according to the divine plan, then conformity comes not as the result of struggle but as the result of happy and joyous submission to the Christ ideal, to the God design. The soul of such a man is always happy and joyous to receive even the little treasures and gifts of divine grace. He searches not of necessity for some great philosophical or theological statement which will exalt his mind within the human domain. He is pleased with the formation of the clouds, with the shape of the leaves upon the trees, with an expression of hope in the eyes of a child or one of ripened years.

He finds not the need to criticize mankind or himself but only to epitomize the divine ideal by loving and joyous obedience to the Christ or God design. Recognizing that he came forth from the Light, he seeks to return to the Light and he desires no longer to walk in the darkness of human reason. Man, then, understands that the anchor that he has cast behind the veil is the anchor that he has sent from his heart and soul as an activity of love unto God. This activity of love flows up the lifestream to the Holy Christ Self and is carried by the consciousness of the Christ back into the heart of the Father.

It is this anchor behind the veil, this deathless sense of identification with God, that enables mankind actually to function at the Divine Monadic level. There, when man functions under divine direction and activity either in or out of the body, he takes the energy dispensed to him which in ignorance might have been misused and creates instead a great body of light called the immaculate seamless garment of the living Christ which will one day become the great spherical Deathless Solar Body.

Born of the energies of the sun and of the energies of the Sun behind the sun, the Deathless Solar Body becomes a magnet. The magnetism of the Divine is a lodestone that will transmute shadow in the human octave and transform the consciousness of the ascendant one so that little by little there will gradually occur in his world a lessening of the tenacious ties which mankind over the centuries have woven to persons, places, conditions, and things. Simultaneously there will occur a renewal of the ancient covenants of the soul with the Father whereby the Son recognizes that the return Home to the heart of God is most imperative.

Thus the divine lodestone and Deathless Solar Body are activated and, because there is a response mechanism created in the consciousness below, it becomes an occasion whereby the Father, through man's own freewill choice, now has the authority to choose the hour when the Son shall return back to himself. Unless, however, the pathway of the flame is created in the caduceus[3] fashion, the soul will not be able to make its winged flight back to God.

The caduceus takes advantage of both centripetal and centrifugal forces. It utilizes the energy known to the Hindus as Brahma and Shiva, the Creator and Destroyer.[4] Thus are mankind made aware of the forces of the negative, or minus, polarity which flow counterclockwise and bring basic structure back to Spirit; and of the forces which flow from Spirit clockwise into the positive realm of manifestation. The caduceus action gives man victory over both hell and death, and with the ascension the last enemy, or death, is destroyed.[5]

The wings at the top of the caduceus symbolize that the holy and vital energies of both sympathetic and central nervous systems around the spinal column have been raised toward the spiritual eye of perception. Here the wings of spiritual perception raise the individual and trigger the cosmic mechanism of the ascension.

Thus the flame above (in the heart of the Presence) magnetizes the flame below (the threefold flame within the heart) and the wedding garment descends around the silver cord to envelop the lifestream of the individual in those tangible and vital essence currents of the ascension. Tremendous changes then take place in the form below, and the four lower bodies of man are cleansed of all impurities. Lighter and lighter grows the physical form, and with the weightlessness of helium the body begins to rise into the atmosphere, the gravitational pull being loosened and the form enveloped by the light of the externalized glory which man knew with the Father "in the beginning" before the world was.

This is the glory of the ascension currents. It is the glory of attainment which Jesus demonstrated on Bethany's hill.[6] This may be experienced by each individual when fifty-one percent of his karma is balanced and he has made the other necessary preparations which make it possible for the Karmic Board to grant that his records be stamped "Candidate for the Ascension." This does not mean an end to life for that individual. Such an individual has been given, as was Elijah in the "chariot of fire,"[7] a glorious means of transport out of human octaves into the octaves of light far above the psychic realm in the heaven world of the ascended masters and cosmic beings.

We shall continue to unfold the greatness of the ascension next week.

Valiantly I AM

Serapis

18

*The Ascension
Must Be Desired*

Unto You Who
Desire Your Ascension
and Desire It Ordinately
It Is Given to Believe
in the Ascended Master
Consciousness Which You
Would Make Your Own
by Your Attention to That
Cosmic Process and Service
Which Will Restore You
to the Former State
That You Knew with God
Before the World Was

Saint Paul long ago said, "Some man will say, How are the dead raised up? and with what body do they come? Thou fool, that which thou sowest is not quickened, except it die:..."[1] His rebuke to the Galatians concerning the following of the letter of the law instead of the Spirit of Christ was also to the point: "O foolish Galatians, who hath bewitched you, that ye should not obey the Truth.... Having begun in the Spirit, are ye now made perfect by the flesh?"[2]

The course of man's victory leading unto his ascension, then, does not come about because of "human goodness" or mankind's pursuit of "accepted social norms." It goes without saying that karma must be balanced. Individuals cannot continue to flaunt the laws of brotherhood and justice; they cannot continue to disobey the infinite laws of God with impunity. It is unrealistic, then, for any man to imagine that he can follow a collision course with the Karmic Board and the heavenly hierarchies by ignoring his spiritual responsibilities and the need to desire the highest gifts and graces which God has already prepared for him.

The ascension must be desired and it must be desired ordinately. It must be desired not as a mechanism of escape from responsibility or from worldly duties. It must be desired as the culmination of a lifetime of service in the will of God, and men must be willing during their final embodiments upon the planet—the time of their escape from the round of the centuries—to give the very best of service to the light and to help usher in the kingdom.

I have known of many individuals who have been so involved in the battle of winning their ascension that they have completely ignored their responsibilities toward their fellowmen and toward the hierarchy. In God's name, beloved ones, you do not need to be like Nero who fiddled while Rome burned. You must take into account the awful treacheries that are abroad in the world today and the extreme pain and suffering in which mankind are enmeshed. Wherever possible, you must seek to draw down into the world the wonderful regenerate energies of the light as a healing afflatus, as an act of mercy and grace, as a joyous experience when you can, by the consummate skill of your Holy Christ Selves and through God's grace, draw forth light in men of lesser understanding.

Let us, then, pinpoint in this dossier the fact that the Brotherhood at Luxor is not seeking to strip the planet of all of its cream. We do not desire to draw to our temple every illumined soul upon earth and then to ascend them all to God, leaving the world bereft of those who hold the balance of light and power and render spiritual assistance unto their fellowmen through the chain of hierarchy. We desire to draw only those whose course

is run and who have recognized that they are near-
ing the fulfillment of their divine plan.

We are also aware of the fact that millions of
people today who have been exposed to the higher teachings through this Dossier on the Ascension
can and will begin to weave patterns of light in
preparation for the fulfillment of their missions in
their final embodiments. Then if they fail in their
present lifespans to reach the mark of the high
calling in Christ,[3] they will have at least, by their
right actions, set the stage of cosmic opportunity
and the cosmic timetable to the point where ad-
justments of a karmic nature will be possible in
their next lifetimes.

The ascension currents can hurt no one. Everyone who receives this flame of regeneration from
the heart of God will understand the need to anchor the ascension currents in his own world
here and now, even as man draws nigh to God by
casting the anchor of his identity beyond the veil of
mortal reckoning into the great sea of God's body
of light. Thus the ascension in the chariot of fire is
always preceded by the magnetization of man's
solar energies which by the consent of his conscious will are raised to the heart of the Divine
Presence.

You need not expect, precious ones, that as
the swoop of a great bird of paradise, heaven will
come down to you and raise you instantly up into
the light. Each day you weave a strand of light
substance back to the heart of your Presence by the
shuttle of your attention; each strand strengthens
the anchor beyond the veil and thus draws you
into a state of consciousness wherein God can use

you more as an effective instrument for good.

Let all understand, then, that the ascension is won just as much by good works and devotion to God, by service to your fellowmen, by service to the light, by decrees offered for and on behalf of mankind, by healing service to those who require it, and by the many avenues of the Brotherhood as it is won by a direct study of the mechanical process involved in the final ritual of the ascension itself.

We have known of a few cases of devotees who spent so much time in studying the mechanics of the ascension and seeking to prepare themselves for that gift that they actually triggered the mechanism of divine grace (for their karma had been fairly well balanced) and they rose prematurely into the ascension only to ask, after having been given this tremendous gift, if they could not then go back down into human form and take care of a bit of unfinished business of which they were made aware. Would it not have been, then, a greater pleasure and joy unto God, as well as man, if those individuals had put first things first, reckoning with their earthly responsibilities and leaving the mechanics of the ascension up to their Divine Presence without seeking to ascend by what we may almost term "violence"? (For the kingdom of heaven suffereth violence, and the violent take it by force.[4])

There are those who say that the end justifies the means, and if they could receive their ascension by getting in an elevator they would do so. We wish to point out that whereas God has provided a very definite pattern for every lifestream and a universal pattern of Christ victory which is commendable to all, there are always exceptions to the rule and these serve only to prove the rule. Thus an individual, having free will, can continue to work and to serve for a given purpose which, while it may be within the keeping and province of the Law, may not necessarily have been the specific intent of the Law for his lifestream in the fulfillment of his mission. Yet because of man's importunity, God will grant that for which he prematurely asks.

This exception in no way contradicts the statement that God knows the hour and the day of man's victory. Man can either thwart the divine plan or he can hasten its fulfillment. The cosmic timetable requires man's attention to process, for by cosmic process and service men are restored to the former state that they knew with God before the world was.[5] Having fulfilled this ritual, they have the added advantage of possessing their entire experience criteria gleaned from many embodiments upon earth which stands before them as an assistance for future service in cosmic realms.

The kingdom of heaven is without end, and lifestreams who enter into their ascension are soon assigned to other tasks in the service of the light. The body of Christ upon earth needs both unascended masters whose very life is wholly dedicated to God and ascended masters who serve mankind without ceasing. There is room in this cosmic scheme for men to play many roles; and the sooner they recognize their need to conform to the divine idea, the quicker they can get on with the business of assisting all the evolutions of life upon this planet to their ultimate freedom.

Heaven always desires to do things the gentle way, to produce the perfection of God into manifestation without the heavy hand of karma being lowered upon humanity. Yet the records clearly show that in many cases only the cosmic hammer was effective in awakening recalcitrant individuals who otherwise would have proceeded to while away their opportunities in indolent and vainglorious activities.

I have covered in this dossier a host of subjects, and the subtleties I have placed between the lines are legion. I hope next week to conclude this dissertation on the ascension, but should I fail to include all that is required for your victory I am certain you will give me audience another week to talk to you about these blessed opportunities of a spiritual nature.

In emulation of the Christ, man may recognize that in relative terms the mission of the Christ—which was thirty-three years of temporary life, thirty being devoted to his early training and three to his final service—created sweeping changes in the world of form and to the present hour has produced untold benefits to the earth. That these benefits are not greater is because of the hardness of men's hearts,[6] which resembles the attitude of Pharaoh in the days when the children of Israel were in bondage. The Mosaic plagues which were brought upon the land of Egypt ultimately shattered the heart of the Pharaoh until he at last relented and let the children go free.[7]

There is much to be learned in the whole divine scheme, and a broken and contrite heart God will not despise.[8] Those who come to him and believe in him must also "believe in me," [9] that is, they must believe in the ascended master consciousness which dwelt not only in Christ, in Jesus, but also abides in every ascended master and will raise thee also to thy mastery that where I AM ye may be also.[10]

For the ages I remain

Serapis

19

The Destiny
of Every Man

Unto the Blessed
Who Are Motivated
by an Absolute Determination
toward Godliness
Is the Cosmic Honor Flame
Fulfilled in the Descent
and the Ascent
of the Father/Mother God
upon the Spinal Altar
As the Victory of the Caduceus
Becomes the Victory
of the Ascension
as the Destiny of
Every Living Soul

We have thought to convey in this dossier the understanding that spiritual exercise alone without obedience to karmic precepts and the divine plan for man may be of limited value to the aspirant. We have also pointed out that both approaches to salvation come to the shining apex of manifestation in man's glorious ascension in the light when all of the spiritual signets are set in place as God wills it. This includes the use of the cosmic honor flame from the heart of God whereby men in honor prefer one another and recognize the meaning of true brotherhood and service.

Again and again we are amazed at the antics of mankind, how they seek spiritual study and spiritual deliverance while creating ever-new attitudes of imperfection and discord toward their brothers. God is never mocked[1] by these false human attitudes which usually attempt to justify themselves by some form of human provocation which may or may not have foundation in fact.

When the honor flame of God is employed men's goals become God oriented, and thus there can be no possibility of deviation or shadow of turning[2] in the human monad who is motivated by an absolute determination toward Godliness. The world is filled with human beings and human creation, but it is to the Divine that men must turn for their freedom. The caduceus action will work twice as effectively in those lifestreams in whom the expression of honor, justice, and mercy go hand in hand with spiritual exercise.

One of the strange little bits of information which I sometimes hesitate to pass on to students because it deals with a process that is almost mechanical is the conveyance of God's energy down to the base of the spinal column and the reversal of that energy back to the heart of the Presence. This process, which has sometimes been used haphazardly by those who are inept in the practice of that which is called *kriyā yoga,* will operate perfectly automatically in those individuals whose devotion to God is great enough.

In the past, many of the saints who levitated into the atmosphere did so by reason of the intensity of their magnetization of the energy of the God flame above. The floating into the air of these saints was an attest to their devout and intimate relationship with the God Presence. Thus the winged God Self will raise man back to His own heart, and that which descended will also ascend.[3] The alchemical marriage (the union of the lower self with the Higher Self) will take place when the lower self has shown good faith and the willingness to fulfill all obligations set forth in the Covenant of Divine Reunion.

Some may say that in the case of an ascension the flesh form will rise, leaving a pile of white ash upon the ground beneath the feet of the aspirant. This is true in some cases where the alchemy of the ascension is performed a bit prematurely and for cosmic reasons. In this instance the white ash is the untransmuted residue of the lifestream. In other cases this residue is absent from the spot where the individual ascended, having been transmuted by an intense caduceus action.

It is true, although the form of an individual may show signs of age prior to his ascension, that all of these signs will change and that the physical appearance of the individual will be transformed into the glorified body. The individual ascends, then, not in an earthly body but in a glorified spiritual body into which the physical form is changed on the instant by total immersion in the great God flame. Thus man's consciousness of the physical body ceases and he achieves a state of weightlessness. This resurrection takes place as the great God flame envelops the shell of human creation that remains and transmutes, in a pattern of cosmic grids, all of the cell patterns of the individual—the bony structure, the blood vessels, and all bodily processes which go through a great metamorphosis.

The blood in the veins changes to liquid golden light; the throat chakra glows with an intense blue-white light; the spiritual eye in the center of the forehead becomes an elongated God flame rising upward; the garments of the individual are completely consumed, and he takes on the appearance of being clothed in a white robe—the seamless garment of the Christ. Sometimes the long hair of the Higher Mental Body appears as pure gold on the ascending one; then again, eyes of any color may become a beautiful electric blue or a pale violet.

These changes are permanent, and the ascended one is able to take his light body with him wherever he wishes or he may travel without the glorified spiritual body. Ascended beings can and occasionally do appear upon earth as ordinary mortals, putting on physical garments resembling the people of earth and moving among them for cosmic purposes. This Saint Germain did after his ascension when he was known as the Wonderman of Europe. Such an activity is a matter of dispensation received from the Karmic Board. Beloved Jesus' appearance before Paul on the road to Damascus is another case in point.[4]

Merely to be carried by the Spirit, as was Philip, from one city to another,[5] or to be raised temporarily into the atmosphere in levitation is not the same as the ascension and should not be so construed. Elijah the prophet, in his ascension, was taken up into heaven in a "chariot of fire."[6] This chariot, so-called, may be actualized or symbolically qualified as the rumbling of the atomic densities of mankind turn as chariot wheels in the fiery substance of the ascension flame until every atom, cell, and electron is purified of all dross. Thus man is propelled into the ascension flame as these "wheels within wheels"[7] are stepped up in vibratory rate until they spin with the intensity of light itself and the divine tone sounds forth from within them the note of individual victory.

Whether it be Zarathustra who ascended back to God in "the great flame," or Elijah who went into heaven in the "chariot of fire"—the flame of the ascension is the key which unlocks the door to immortality for every man. The flame is the vehicle which conveys the ascended one back to the heart of his Divine Presence. He retains full consciousness of this entire ritual and, once ascended, he becomes on the instant an emissary of the Great White Brotherhood in carrying out its various aims which always come under the direction of the Fatherhood of God.

Life is a closed corporation. If God is the chairman of this board, then Christ is the president and the board of directors are the ascended masters and the Karmic Board. Heaven can be justly said to be a closed union shop where no one can actually work against the divine aims. Although man has chosen to rebel against the will of God and has walked in darkness and in ignorance, although many have professed to be great souls, avatars, or spiritual beings of great power, the reality of that power is determined by the eternal Spirit of God, and illumination and grace are conveyed to *every* lifestream through the Spirit of the living Christ.

The ascension is an inevitable part of the divine system. It consists of these initiations: the transfiguration into the divine configuration, the ritual of crucifixion upon the cross of Matter, the resurrection from dead substance, and, at last, that of the ascension flame itself which raises man out of the domain of his recalcitrant energies and all treacherous activities, mortal imperfection and error. The ascension is the beginning of the kingdom for each one; and when every soul is taken and none left, the world itself will ascend back to the heart of God, a planet victorious.

To this end must we work and serve. The pyramid of cosmic truth, builded on lively stones,[8] must rise from the great plains of Mamre (Mamray, symbolizing the Motherhood of God which endows the planes of Matter, Mater, as the launching platform of the soul's ascension).[9] The Eternal Mother must shield the Eternal Son. The shell of cosmic purity must trumpet forth the victory of man in accordance with the divine plan. The course of life may wend its way over a variegated terrain and under a multitude of circumstances, but when the stream becomes crystal clear and purified, it merges with the sea of glass— the cosmic cube of perfection, the white stone that signifies that purpose, ideal, and action have been purified in man.[10]

The divine geometry, through the symbol of the pyramid, draws the aspiring consciousness of man into the idea of an ascendant life. To ascend is to blend in cosmic unity with the heart of the Eternal. It is the destiny of every man. Those who understand this will rejoice in the consolation of their own ultimate freedom from every earthly travail as cosmic purpose is enthroned in consciousness both now and forever. My hands will be extended in loving welcome to thee at the hour of thy victory.

I remain your teacher and friend,

Serapis Bey

Notes

For an alphabetical listing of many of the philosophical and hierarchical terms used in *Dossier on the Ascension*, see the comprehensive glossary, "The Alchemy of the Word: Stones for the Wise Masterbuilders," in *Saint Germain On Alchemy*.

CHAPTER 1

1. I Sam. 17:50.
2. Isa. 40:3; Matt. 3:3.
3. Prov. 22:6.
4. (Dan. 7:9) The name "Ancient of Days" refers to Sanat Kumara, who came to the Earth millions of years ago when the planet was at her darkest hour. He volunteered to hold the focus of the flame of life until her evolutions would once again draw forth enough energy from God to sustain life. On January 1, 1956, Gautama Buddha, his first disciple, assumed the office of Lord of the World.
5. I Cor. 15:31.
6. Rev. 22:2.
7. Mark 8:24.
8. Matt. 22:11, 12.
9. Exod. 3:14.
10. Matt. 7:15, 16.
11. I Cor. 13:1.
12. Eph. 5:26.
13. Matt. 18:10.
14. I Cor. 15:52.
15. Rom. 12:9.

CHAPTER 2

1. *Hamlet,* act 3, sc. 1, lines 65-68.
2. Pss. 16:10; Acts 2:27.
3. I Cor. 15:56.
4. Pss. 51:5.
5. Luke 1:78.
6. I Cor. 15:47.
7. Pss. 82:6; John 10:34.
8. Rom. 3:12.

9. Matt. 15:14.
10. Acts 1:9.
11. Col. 3:3.
12. Luke 2:14, 11.
13. I John 1:5.
14. Rom. 8:17.
15. Exod. 13:21, 22.
16. John 14:3.

CHAPTER 3

1. I Cor. 3:19.
2. Miguel de Cervantes, *Don Quixote* (1605, 1615).

CHAPTER 4

1. Heb. 12:6.
2. Matt. 6:24.
3. Matt. 13:45, 46.
4. II Chron. 32:8; Jer. 17:5.
5. James 4:6; I Pet. 5:5.
6. Prov. 16:18.

CHAPTER 5

1. Gen. 11:6, 7.
2. Gen. 3:24.
3. John 1:3.
4. I Cor. 2:9.
5. Rev. 13:16-18.
6. *AUM, OM* (H-ome), Sanskrit word which carries the approximate light vibration of the English words Amen or "I AM"; the name of God.
7. Matt. 23:27, 28.
8. II Pet. 3:10.
9. That stratum of the earth also known as the emotional or psychic plane where the sewer of mankind's mass effluvic patterns accumulate and where souls of lesser advancement gravitate after they pass from the physical screen of life—not having enough light to propel them to higher octaves and the masters' etheric temples.
10. Eph. 4:10.

CHAPTER 6

1. Gen. 1:2.
2. John 10:30.
3. Matt. 19:28.
4. Matt. 6:23.
5. II Tim. 2:15.
6. I Cor. 15:26.
7. Rom. 12:19.

CHAPTER 7

1. Rom. 8:7.
2. Gen. 25:29-34.
3. Matt. 6:24.
4. I Cor. 2:9.
5. Matt. 22:21.
6. Gen. 15:1.
7. John 18:36.
8. II Tim. 3:5.
9. Acts 16:31.
10. John 3:16.
11. Luke 17:21.

CHAPTER 8

1. II Tim. 2:15.
2. Rev. 10:9, 10.
3. Num. 22.
4. John 20:25, 29.
5. Mark 10:15; Luke 18:17.
6. I Cor. 3:13.
7. Luke 23:34.
8. Pss. 23:1-3.

CHAPTER 9

1. Ezek. 12:2.
2. Matt. 7:2; I Chron. 16:34.
3. I Cor. 15:52.
4. Pss. 52:1.
5. Matt. 7:13, 14.
6. Matt. 8:12; 22:13; 25:30.

CHAPTER 10

1. Gen. 1:27, 28.
2. *Rubáiyát of Omar Khayyám* (trans. Edward FitzGerald, 5th ed.), quatrain 71. Note: "O Mark, I AM!"

CHAPTER 11

1. Heb. 11:6.
2. I Tim. 6:10.
3. Matt. 10:28.
4. Matt. 24:35; 5:18.

CHAPTER 12

1. Heb. 12:29.
2. Heb. 6:1; 9:14.
3. I Cor. 3:16; 6:19.
4. I Cor. 15:50.
5. Matt. 13:35.
6. Pss. 1:1.

CHAPTER 13

1. Matt. 5:8.
2. I Cor. 15:26, 55.
3. Luke 15:11-32.

CHAPTER 14

1. Rev. 15:2; 21:18-21.
2. Gen. 4:9.
3. This is a reference to the law of octaves which gives the evolutions that abide in the physical octave complete dominion in the world of form, even as the ascended masters are the authority in their octave. Through the use of their free will, in the name of God, mankind can invoke and immediately receive the assistance of the ascended masters in their domain. Without this invitation the masters are not permitted, by cosmic law, to intervene in the affairs of men. One of the problems which modern theology has not been able to answer satisfactorily is the question posed by many sincere seekers: "Why does God allow so much evil in the world?" The answer is that the children of God as a whole have

not asked for help enough—they have not invoked the assistance of the heavenly hosts in enough numbers to counteract the forces of evil that have been allowed (by humanity's misuse of their free will) to run rampant on the world scene.

4. Heb. 10:7.
5. Hab. 2:2.

CHAPTER 15

1. Matt. 18:3.

CHAPTER 16

1. The "Prince of the Realm" is your own beloved Holy Christ Self who, when given (by the correct application of your own free will) the "reign" of authority to govern the realm of the lower consciousness, will unlock the door to a cornucopia of divine blessings from on high.

2. "There is no weapon more deadly than the will." F. Max Muller, ed., *The Sacred Books of the East* (Oxford: Clarendon Press, 1879-1910), vol. 40, "The Writings of Kwang-Tze," *The Texts of Taoism,* trans. James Legge (1891), p. 84.

3. Luke 2:14.
4. Mark 4:39.
5. Matt. 22:11-14.

CHAPTER 17

1. Matt. 22:11-14.
2. See the Chart of Your Divine Self for a more vivid understanding of this process.
3. A herald's wand, and hence the staff used by messengers. The caduceus of Hermes is a familiar example. In its oldest form, it was a rod ending in two prongs (probably an olive branch with two shoots, adorned with ribbons or garlands) for which, later, two serpents with heads meeting at the top were substituted. A pair of wings was sometimes attached to the top of the staff. In historical times, the caduceus was the attribute of Hermes as the god of commerce and peace; and among the Greeks, it was the distinctive mark of heralds and ambassadors, whose persons it rendered inviolable. *Encyclopedia Britannica,* s.v. "caduceus."
4. The Hindu Trinity—Brahma, the Creator; Vishnu, the Preserver; and Shiva, the Destroyer.

5. I Cor. 15:26.
6. Acts 1:9.
7. II Kings 2:11.

CHAPTER 18

1. I Cor. 15:35, 36. Paul's reference is clarified in Jesus' own words as recorded by John: "Verily, verily, I say unto you, Except a corn of wheat fall into the ground and die, it abideth alone: but if it die, it bringeth forth much fruit. He that loveth his life shall lose it; and he that hateth his life in this world shall keep it unto life eternal" (John 12:24, 25).
2. Gal. 3:1, 3.
3. Phil. 3:14.
4. Matt. 11:12.
5. John 17:5.
6. Mark 16:14.
7. Exod. 7-12.
8. Pss. 51:17.
9. This statement clarifies the following Biblical passages: John 6:29-40; 10:9; 11:25-27; 14:1; Acts 8:37; 16:31; 19:4; Rom. 10:9-13; I John 3:23-24.
10. John 14:3.

CHAPTER 19

1. Gal. 6:7.
2. James 1:17.
3. Eph. 4:9, 10.
4. Acts 9:3-5.
5. Acts 8:26-39.
6. II Kings 2:11.
7. Ezek. 1:16.
8. I Pet. 2:5.
9. Gen. 18:1.
10. Rev. 15:2; 22:1; 2:17.

You are invited by Beloved Serapis Bey to offer in full voice these two dynamic decrees for soul purification which are given by all initiates at Luxor. They are included for your Communion with the Saints Ascended, the Body of God in heaven, through the Science of the Spoken Word.

Prayer for Purity

In the name of the beloved mighty victorious Presence of God, I AM in me, my very own beloved Holy Christ Self, I call to the heart of the Saviour Jesus Christ and the servant-sons of God who are with him in heaven—beloved Serapis Bey and the Brotherhood at Luxor, beloved Archangel Gabriel, beloved Justinius and the great seraphim and cherubim, beloved Elohim of Purity and Astrea, beloved Lanello, the entire Spirit of the Great White Brotherhood and the World Mother:

Beloved Serapis, in God's name I AM
Calling for Purity's ray to expand,
Imploring that shadows no longer adhere,
So longing for Purity now to appear.

My mind purify of its fleeting impression,
My feelings release of all impure direction;
Let memory retain the immaculate concept
And treasure the pearl of the Holy Christ precept.

O souvenir of radiant wonder,
Let my mind on thee now ponder;
Christ discrimination, sunder
   All that's less than God-success!

Cut me free from all deception,
Fix my mind on pure perception;
Hear, O thou, my invocation—
   My Christ Self to manifest!

O flame of cosmic purity,
From Luxor, blaze through me;
Completely clear all shadowed weights,
   Ascend me now to thee!

Give ending "And in full faith. . . ." See p. 114.

Communion with the Cosmic Consciousness of
The Golden Pink Glow Ray
and the Saints Who Ensoul It

In the name of the beloved mighty victorious Presence of God, I AM in me, and my very own beloved Holy Christ Self, I call to the heart of the Saviour Jesus Christ and the servant-sons of God who are with him in heaven—beloved Serapis Bey and the Brotherhood at Luxor, beloved Archangel Gabriel, beloved Elohim of Purity and Astrea, beloved Justinius and the great seraphim and cherubim, beloved Sanat Kumara, the Ancient of Days, Lord Gautama, Lord Maitreya, beloved Saint Germain, the cosmic beings Harmony and Victory, Helios and Vesta, the seven mighty Elohim, the seven beloved archangels, the seven beloved chohans of the rays, beloved Lanello, the entire Spirit of the Great White Brotherhood and the World Mother:

1. I AM calling today for thy golden pink ray
   To manifest round my form.
   Golden pink light, dazzling bright,
   My four lower bodies adorn!

Refrain: O Brotherhood at Luxor and
      blessed Serapis Bey
   Hear our call and answer by
      love's ascending ray.
   Charge, charge, charge our being
   With essence pure and bright;
   Let thy hallowed radiance
   Of ascension's mighty light
   Blaze its dazzling light rays
   Upward in God's name,
   Till all of heaven claims us
   For God's ascending flame.

2. Saturate me with golden pink light,
   Make my four lower bodies bright;
   Saturate me with ascension's ray,
   Raise my four lower bodies today!

3. Surround us now with golden pink love
   Illumined and charged with light from above;
   Absorbing this with lightning speed,
   I AM fully charged with Victory's mead.

Give ending "And in full faith. . . ." See p. 114.

Index

FOR MORE INFORMATION

For a free catalog of books and tapes on the teachings of the Ascended Masters or for information about Summit University retreats, weekend seminars and quarterly conferences, Elizabeth Clare Prophet's cable TV shows, the Keepers of the Flame Fraternity, or the Ascended Masters' library and study center nearest you, write or call: The Summit Lighthouse, Box 5000, Livingston, Montana 59047-5000. Telephone: (406) 222-8300.

Since 1958 Mark L. Prophet and Elizabeth Clare Prophet have written such classics of spiritual literature as *The Lost Years of Jesus, The Lost Teachings of Jesus, Climb the Highest Mountain, The Human Aura, Saint Germain On Alchemy, The Science of the Spoken Word* and *Forbidden Mysteries of Enoch.* They have also lectured in over 30 countries.

In 1970 the Prophets founded Montessori International and in 1971 Summit University. Mark Prophet passed on in 1973 and Mrs. Prophet has carried on their work. She is based at the Royal Teton Ranch in southwestern Montana, home of a spiritual community.

Here Mrs. Prophet conducts seminars and workshops on the practical applications of the mystical paths of the world's religions. Cable TV shows based on these teachings air weekly across the United States. Mrs. Prophet also appears frequently on national television and has talked about her work on "Donahue," "Larry King Live!" "Nightline," "Sonya Live" and "CNN & Company."